LIFE
SKILLS

LIFE SKILLS
HOW TO DO
ALMOST ANYTHING

Chicago Tribune

MIDWAY

AN AGATE IMPRINT

CHICAGO

Illustrations by Rick Tuma except on pages 49, 95, and 159 (illustrations on those pages by Casey Millard).

Chicago Tribune
Tony W. Hunter, Publisher
Gerould W. Kern, Editor
R. Bruce Dold, Editorial Page Editor
Bill Adee, Vice President/Digital
Jane Hirt, Managing Editor
Joycelyn Winnecke, Associate Editor
Peter Kendall, Deputy Managing Editor

Printed in the United States of America.

Library of Congress Cataloging-in-Publication Data

Life skills : how to do almost anything / edited by the Chicago Tribune Staff.
    pages cm
  Includes bibliographical references and index.
  Summary: "A collection of articles from the Chicago Tribune's 'Life Skills' column"-- Provided by publisher.
   ISBN 978-1-57284-149-9 (pbk.) -- ISBN 1-57284-149-4 (pbk.) -- ISBN 978-1-57284-420-9 (ebook) --   ISBN 1-57284-420-5 (ebook)
  1. Life skills--Handbooks, manuals, etc. 2. Home economics--Handbooks, manuals, etc. 3. Etiquette. I. Chicago Tribune (Firm)
  HQ2037.L55 2013
  646.7--dc23
                                    2013019119

10 9 8 7 6 5 4 3 2 1

Midway is an imprint of Agate Publishing. Agate books are available in bulk at discount prices. For more information visit agatepublishing.com.

CONTENTS

BASICS

AT THE OFFICE

PLAY

TECHNICAL

SOCIAL

BASICS

Arrange Flowers

Before launching her fearlessflowers.com, Annie Vanderwarker commissioned a survey. It found that 68 percent of people who bought cut flowers at the grocery store were afraid to arrange them. "They just plunk them in something without even trying to arrange them," she says. But with a little forethought and effort, a merely adequate arrangement can become a real eye-catcher. And Vanderwarker is willing to help.

STEP 1: PLANNING
Before you snip your first stem, think it out. What is this arrangement for and where is it going?

PLACEMENT
If it's a centerpiece at a dinner table: Don't exceed 12 inches in height; you don't want guests having to peer through a jungle to see the person across the table. If the arrangement will sit against a wall, flowers face outward, in one direction. No need to put on a 360-degree show.

CONTAINER

First, choose between glass and ceramic. If you're worried about how your stems will look and don't want to incorporate them in the finished work, go ceramic. There are vases in every size and shape. If you're worried your flowers won't stand at attention, create a grid across the top of the vase using tape (florist's tape or even scotch tape will work).

STEPS 2 & 3: SELECTING & CUTTING

SELECTING

If you're cutting your own, do it early in the morning because they don't like to be cut during the heat of the day. But flowers from a grocery store's floral department—this is what most people have easy access to, Vanderwarker points out—will work just fine. There is a huge variety to choose from. The most popular are roses, carnations, tulips and gerbera daisies, she says. And you don't need a lot; An attractive arrangement can be made with three to five flowers.

For an interesting change, there are some flowers that do well underwater and can last more than a week. Hydrangea, tulips, orchids and anything else with a kind of a waxy surface will work. Making it more interesting: The flowers get magnified by the glass container.

Flowers that last longer include alstroemeria, tulips and sunflowers. Two points to remember: Tulips will continue to grow after you've put them in a container, and you can eliminate the awkwardness of tall sunflowers—everybody loves them but not everyone knows how to make them look good—by cutting the stems or by weaving them together.

As for colors, it's up to you.

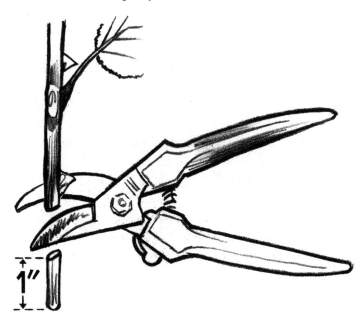

CUTTING

Trim an inch or two off every stem with a clean cut. If it's a woody stem—hydrangea, for example—split the stem at the bottom. It'll help the absorption of water.

Vanderwarker suggests some overnight prep work on the gerbera daisies. She puts a baker's cooling rack over a bucket of water and stands the daisies in the water, up to their necks. The additional water pulled up by the flower will make it stand up better.

STEP 4: ARRANGING

If it's a tight arrangement or if you've got a tape grid across the top, put the water—room temperature—in the vase first. If it's a loose arrangement, the water can go in afterward.

"I usually try to add flower food, the one that comes one pre-packaged at the grocery store," Vanderwarker says, "or a couple of drops of bleach." (Bleach kills bacteria, which can inhibit the flowers' absorption of water.)

Strip any leaves that would be underwater; they'd just rot and foul the water.

Don't be afraid to shorten the flowers. Many vases are v-shaped to take advantage of a big bunch of flowers. But if the flowers are tall, they can spread over and flop over. Vanderwark-er prefers square and rectangular containers. Also remember: The closer the heads are to the edge of the container, the fewer flowers you'll need. So shorten them up.

It usually doesn't matter what order to place the flowers in the vase. "If I'm using (a lot of) flowers, usually I take the ones that have the woodiest stems or ones with the most support structure first (so) I can balance the others with them."

Clean a Bathroom

It's a dirty job—but someone's got to clean the bathroom. And when it's you, what's the most efficient way?

Since most materials used in bathrooms are easy to clean, give it a quick wipe daily, experts advise. Tackle a full clean once a week.

"Frequent cleanings mean less work because there will not be weeks of crud to clean," says Cathy Faulcon Bowen, a professor with Pennsylvania State University's department of agricultural and extension education. "If you have a single bathroom and many users, the bathroom might need to be cleaned more often."

DEGREE OF DIFFICULTY: Easy. Less elbow grease than hand-washing your car.

TIME COMMITMENT: 5 minutes daily; 30 minutes once a week

WHAT YOU NEED: Cloth or sponge, rubber gloves, all-purpose cleaner, baking soda, glass cleaner, long-handled toilet bowl brush, bucket

DAILY

- Rinse out sink, bathtub and shower stall after each use.
- Remove excess hair from sink or tub.
- Flush toilet after each use.
- Hang up towels and washcloths.
- Remove dirty clothes.

WEEKLY

STEP 1: EVERYTHING BUT THE TOILET

- Swab sink/tub/shower stall. Wash these areas with a soapy cloth or sponge and all-purpose cleaner; rinse with clear water.
- Clean the space behind water faucet controls and backsplash: Soap scum can accumulate at fixtures' edges. "To clean this tight area well, you usually have to use an old toothbrush," Bowen says.
- Cleaning tip: Use baking soda and wet sponge to clean scum or stubborn marks; rinse with clear water.
- Most plastic shower curtains can be machine-washed with a load of towels (check the tag). Hang wet shower curtain in the bathroom to air dry.
- Shine mirror with glass cleaner.

Clean the Refrigerator

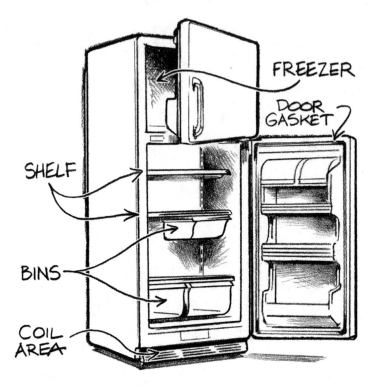

FREEZER

DOOR GASKET

SHELF

BINS

COIL AREA

It is America's dirty, sticky, smelly, well-chilled secret: Our refrigerators are not as clean as they should be. "The refrigerator is a spot in the house where it's easy to accumulate stuff," says Carolyn Forte, director of home appliances and cleaning products at the Good Housekeeping Research Institute. "People put things in. You go to a restaurant, and you get takeout; you shove that in. Things have a way of working their way to the back and never coming out again." Here's Forte's approach to cleaning:

WHAT YOU NEED: 30 minutes, hot water, liquid dish detergent, sponge, soft cloths or paper towels for drying. "You really don't need any strong chemical cleaners; you don't need any tough abrasive tools or sponges."

STEP 1

Clean out the refrigerator. "Get rid of old food you're not going to use, things way past their prime," says Forte. Wipe drips and condensation off jars and bottles.

STEP 2

Do one shelf at a time; temporarily move items to another shelf. Tackling the whole thing? Move items to a counter. If cleaning takes longer than 30 minutes (it shouldn't), consider using a cooler.

STEP 3

Mix hot water and dishwashing liquid in the sink. Start with the main shelves; they're generally removable, so take them out and put them in the dishwater. Wash, rinse, dry and put back. Can't remove them? Wash with a soft cloth or sponge and soapy water, rinse and wipe dry.

STEP 4

Bins generally come out; wash, rinse, dry and put back. Check and clean places that collect drips: behind and under the bins. Pull out drawers; check the runners of the drawers. Wipe bins on the door.

STEP 5

"It's a good thing to give the gasket around the door a cleaning with the soap and water," says Forte. "You want to make sure nothing grows in the crevices. You don't want any mold in there."

STEP 6

Cover food well and return to refrigerator. Since "air circulates between the refrigerator and the freezer, sometimes if your ice smells, it's because food is not covered well."

STEP 7

Wipe down the exterior using all-purpose cleaner (or a stainless steel cleaner for a stainless steel refrigerator). Pay attention to the handles. Clean the top of the refrigerator (if it's not built in), a magnet for greasy soil.

STEP 8

Vacuum out dust or use a brush to clean the coils according to your manual (many refrigerator manuals are now online). If you have an ice and water dispenser, make sure you change filter.

TIPS

- GUNK: If anything's stuck on, rinse a cloth in really hot water, lay it on that stuck-on residue for a while; that generally softens it, and you can remove it.

- BINS: Consider lining bins with a paper towel. "If the lettuce gets wilted or something gets moldy, just toss it away," says Forte. Replace with a fresh one to help things stay clean.

PAPER TOWEL LINER

BIN

- CLEAN: For more cleaning tips, check out Good Housekeeping's iPhone app, Good Housekeeping @Home

- TOSS: For guidelines, go to stilltasty.com

Cut Your Own Hair

Although it's best to leave the pixie cut or layered bob to the pros, amateurs can perform a basic trim if they need to save on a salon visit or cannot tolerate their split ends one moment longer. Elena De Vera, master stylist at Avant Garde Salon and Spa in Miami, offered tips for trimming your tresses.

DEGREE OF DIFFICULTY: Medium. (If you've never done this, it requires a certain level of bravado. But remember: Your hair will grow back.)

WHAT YOU NEED: Comb, sharp scissors, clean, dry hair—only the pros should cut hair when wet

TO TRIM DEAD ENDS OR OVERALL LENGTH

Part your hair down the middle, and bring each side forward as though you're making pigtails. Brush one side evenly and thoroughly with a comb, and stretch it until it's taut.

Slide your middle and index fingers to where you wish to cut, keeping all the hair from the back between your fingers, and cut straight across, just underneath your fingers. Then do the other side.

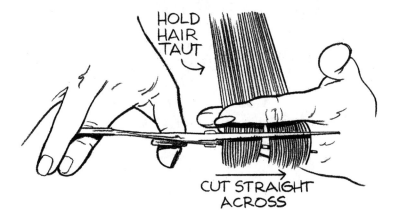

HOLD HAIR TAUT

CUT STRAIGHT ACROSS

TO TRIM FRONT LAYERS (FOR LONG LAYERS—CUT-TING SHORT LAYERS IS TOO EASY TO MESS UP)

With hair parted in the middle, comb the shortest layer out and hold it in front of your face between your middle and index finger. Following the line that already exists, snip toward the hair, so that the point of the scissors is facing the ends. Do half an inch to start; you can always cut more if it isn't enough. Do the next shortest layer, and so on.

Note: Cutting hair while it's parted in the middle gives you the most flexibility for styling, but you can cut it at your regular part if you know you'll always wear it that way.

TO TRIM BANGS

Comb bangs out, grasp them in your hand and twist them once or twice. With scissors pointing up, cut into the hairs vertically just under your eyebrow line for a soft, wispy bang.

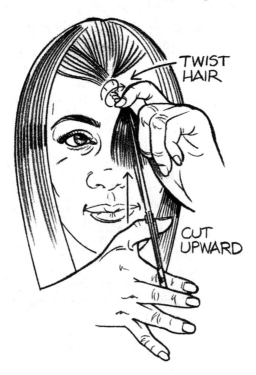

To create side-swept bangs, angle bangs down, with the shortest bangs hitting the top of the outermost part of your eyebrow, and the longest bangs hitting where your cheekbone meets your hairline on the other side of your face. Start on the side where you want bangs to be shortest and cut vertically into the hairs; work your way down toward the longer side. Use a ruler as a visual guide before cutting, or place Scotch tape along your desired bang line to keep you in line.

TO TRIM SHORT HAIR

It's best to leave short hair to the pros, but if you want to just clean up around the ears: Lift and comb the hair out so that it's parallel to the floor, and cut into it (point of scissors toward the hair), following the existing lines.

ABOUT CUTTING DIRECTLY INTO THE ENDS:

- Yes, you'll miss some hairs cutting this way, but that's the

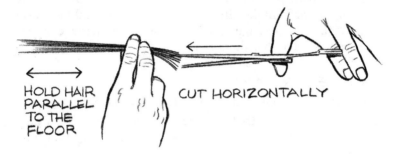

HOLD HAIR PARALLEL TO THE FLOOR

CUT HORIZONTALLY

point: When you do a blunt cut it can create an effect that's too heavy looking.

- Cutting into the hair is not recommended for very curly hair or for African-American hair. In those cases, it's best to cut straight across.

Decode Nutritional Labels

The Nutrition facts label tells you what's in your favorite foods. But if you lose your train of thought somewhere between "servings per container" and "total carbohydrate," Sarah Krieger, a spokesperson for the American Dietetic Association, is here to help with understand some of the key ingredients.

SERVING SIZE & DAILY VALUES

SERVING SIZE: If your iced tea says 100 calories per serving and one serving per container, you're downing 100 calories per bottle. If your iced tea says 100 calories per serving and 2.5 servings per container, that's 250 calories per bottle.

DAILY VALUES: The FDA uses daily value to tell you how much of each element you should consume each day relative to your overall caloric intake. The label is based on a 2,000-calorie diet. (Larger packaging, below, has recommended maximums based on two diets.)

CALORIES FROM FAT

Some foods—peanut butter, salad dressing—should be nearly all fat. But if you see that your 300-calorie frozen dinner gets 200 of its calories from fat, that's a red flag. Check the list of ingredients to determine what kinds of fat are in the food. Hydrogenated and partly hydrogenated fats should be avoided. Vegetable oils are a better choice.

TRANS FAT: No daily value established by FDA, but trans fat is linked to raising bad cholesterol levels. Avoid.

CARBS, FIBER

A lot of people look at carbohydrates, a category that can be confusing because it includes both natural and added sugars. Krieger prefers to check out fiber. For adults the daily goal is 25 to 35 grams, so if you get 3 grams per serving from bread that's pretty good.

KIDS: They need less fiber; the guideline is "age plus 5," so if your child is 3, she needs a minimum of 8 grams of fiber a day.

SODIUM

Guidelines for sodium are in flux, with American Heart Association now saying that less than 1500 milligrams a day is the goal. That's a very small amount of salt by American standards— less than a teaspoon. So look at the milligrams of sodium on the label and ask yourself, is it going to make me exceed my daily goal?

CALCIUM

Don't stress out over Vitamins A and C; most Americans get enough. Iron, similarly, is not as critical as it once was, due to factors such as the fortification of cereal. Calcium is the only vitamin/mineral Krieger is really concerned about, especially in the case of, say, a yogurt with a lot of added sugar.

SUGAR

No daily reference value has been established for sugars because no recommendations have been made for the total amount to eat in a day.

PROTEIN

Current scientific evidence indicates that protein intake is not a public health concern for adults and children over 4 years of age. Eat all you want.

Hang a Painting

Hanging a painting is an art in itself, though you can hardly plead creative license when it's too high, crooked and resting amid a bed of misplaced nail holes. For the sake of your sanity—and your poor walls—home improvement expert Danny Lipford, host of the syndicated TV show "Today's Homeowner With Danny Lipford" (dannylipford.com), offered tips for hanging a painting right the first time.

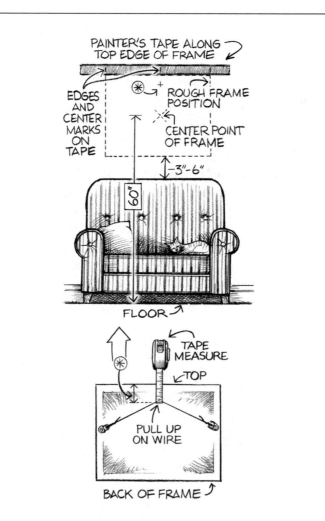

PAINTER'S TAPE ALONG TOP EDGE OF FRAME

EDGES AND CENTER MARKS ON TAPE

ROUGH FRAME POSITION

CENTER POINT OF FRAME

—3"–6"

60"

FLOOR

TAPE MEASURE

TOP

PULL UP ON WIRE

BACK OF FRAME

LIFE SKILLS | BASICS   25

WHAT YOU NEED: Painting (framed, with hanging wire affixed to the back), hammer, picture hooks and nails or threaded anchors with screws, measuring tape, painter's tape, level, pencil

DEGREE OF DIFFICULTY: Fairly easy, provided you pay attention to details.

TIPS ON PLACEMENT

- The rule of thumb is to hang art at eye level, with the center about 60 inches above the floor.

- When hanging art above furniture, leave at least 3 to 6 inches of wall space above a sofa and 4 to 8 inches above a table. The art should be centered over the furniture if the furniture isn't centered on the wall.

- Hang small pieces in clusters to avoid their appearing to be floating on a vast wall. The grouping then becomes the artwork.

- Hang multiple, different-size pieces so that the centers are aligned; the tops and bottoms of the frames don't have to line up.

- Leave 4 to 6 inches between paintings.

STEP 1

Measure about 60 inches up from the floor; mark the wall with a pencil. (Don't worry about finding a wall stud unless the piece weighs more than 40 pounds.)

STEP 2

Center the painting over the mark. Affix a strip of painter's tape to the wall along where the top edge of the frame will be. Use a level to ensure the tape is straight. Mark each end of the frame on the tape; set painting aside.

STEP 3

Measure width of the painting, divide by two and mark the middle point on the tape. That mark will help you locate the best place to hammer in a nail if you use one hanger. (If you plan to use two hangers, which is a good idea for wider frames that need extra stability, mark the points equidistant from the middle point to the edges of the frame.)

STEP 4

Turn painting over; measure the distance from the top of the wire—pulled taut as if it's hanging—to the top of the frame. If you want to hang from two hooks, pull up from the wire at two equidistant points simultaneously and measure to the top of the frame.

STEP 5

Measure that distance down from the bottom edge of the painter's tape, and mark the wall. Again, use a level to make sure your wall mark (or marks) will be plumb with the marks on the strip of tape.

STEP 6

Place the bottom of the hook at the wall mark; hammer it in. For a light painting, a 6 penny (2-inch) nail hammered in at an angle will do. For more support, use a screw with a threaded anchor.

STEP 7

To keep the painting from shifting, put a small dot of picture putty on the bottom corners of the back of the frame. The friction of the putty against the wall helps keep the painting straight. Look good? Remove the painter's tape.

Iron a Shirt

Surely, there will come a moment in your life when the only thing that stands between you and whatever it is you covet (job interview/hot date/big meeting/you name it) is the wrinkled mess that is your only clean shirt. To assist, we called on Gwen Whiting, co-founder of The Laundress (laundry accoutrements at thelaundress.com). She's got a degree in textile science from the Ivy League, and was actually graded for ironing.

STEP 1: PREP
Check for grime on the bottom of the iron. Also clear the ironing board of any debris. If it's really dusty, throw the cover in the wash.

STEP 2: START WET
Skip the dryer, ironing straight from the washing machine. Not possible? Use a spray bottle of water to dampen.

HEAT: Crank iron to whatever temp matches your shirt. Look for the itty-bitty words on the dial and on the back of your shirt tag. If your shirt is oxford cloth, crank to "cotton/linen."

STEP 3: STARCH?
It's optional and builds up over time, so you should occasionally throw the shirt in the wash to remove build-up, even if you usually dry clean.

TYPES: Corn starch is for natural fabrics; sizing for synthetic fabrics. Spray on before ironing begins.

STEP 4: COLLAR & CUFFS
COLLAR: Pop it and iron from the tips toward the middle. Iron the inside. Flip. Do the outside. Don't turn down the collar until the rest of the shirt is ironed. Do NOT iron a crease into the collar.

CUFFS: Starting on the inside, iron from bottom edge toward the sleeve. Flip cuff. Repeat. Also poke the tip of the iron into the pleat(s) just above the cuff.

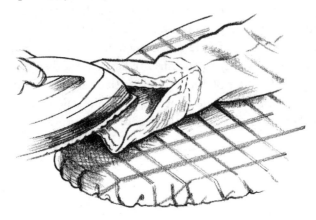

STEP 5: SLEEVES & YOKE

SLEEVES: Hold up and tug taut the arm so you've got a crisp straight fold from shoulder to cuff. Lay sleeve on the board, and in long sweeping strokes, iron in a straight solid crease. Do the back of the sleeve first because inevitably you'll get creases, so save the front for last. Slide the armpit part of the sleeve over the tip of the ironing board, and iron flat the shoulder.

YOKE: Staying in that position, hit the yoke, that double-layer strip that connects the collar to the shirt body. Swing the iron from shoulder to mid-back. Switch shoulders. Repeat.

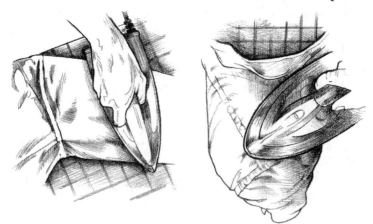

STEP 6: TRUNK, BACK, FRONT & DONE

- **FRONT NON-BUTTON SIDE:** In long strokes from collar down, start with the placket (the strip with all the button holes).

- **POCKET:** Iron from the bottom up.

- **BACK:** Iron below the yoke, from top to bottom.

- **FRONT BUTTON-SIDE:** Lastly, using the tip of the iron, weave in and around the buttons.

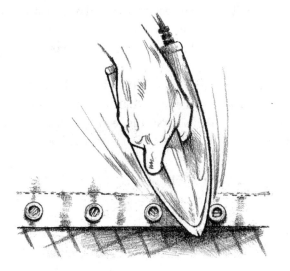

- **DONE:** Hang it up so as not to have to do it again (wooden hanger preferred).

Make a Good Sign

It's a mystery why somebody will spend days or weeks gathering items for a yard sale, clean them up, price them, carefully display them, then announce the sale with a slapdash sign that looks like an afterthought. Similarly, a FOR SALE BY OWNER sign that looks like it was scribbled by a chimp isn't going to attract prospective buyers.

A good sign conveys a message and gets attention. It's worth the effort to do it right.

WHAT YOU NEED: Poster board, wide-tipped marker

DEGREE OF DIFFICULTY: Easy

THE MEDIUM

You need something with heft that looks professional. A piece of notebook paper is too flimsy. Invest in poster board. Neon pink or green will show up best; yellow and orange are also good choices. Stick with the same color for all your signs (and put one, with similarly hued balloons, in front of your house to extend the message).

Use black ink for contrast. Write in large block letters with a thick-tipped marker. Remember that neatness counts. (If neatness is beyond you, hardware stores sell large block adhesive letters and stencils with which you can compose your sign.)

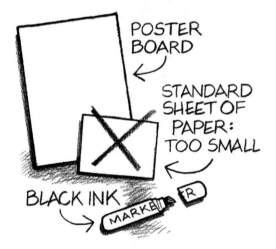

THE MESSAGE

Keep it to a minimum. Less information = more room for type. Bigger type is easier to read, especially for somebody driving by.

One thing to leave off the sign is your address. Unless potential customers (or "suckers," depending on what you're trying to unload) know the neighborhood, a random address is meaningless. Instead, include a big arrow pointing them in the right direction. Check periodically to make sure your sign has stayed put.

Consider the wording. YARD SALE may be fine, but isn't MOVING SALE better? More immediacy, even a whiff of desperation.

PLACEMENT

You can nail your signs to neighborhood utility poles, but some cities have forbidden such displays of entrepreneurship. There's no point posting signs that will be summarily yanked down by power-mad authorities. Then what will you do with all those eight-track tapes?

After your next local election, doublecheck the local rules governing any leftover political signs that blight the landscape. According to Matt Samp, an owner of candidatesigns.com, if they're on public property and are considered litter and are targeted for recycling, you can grab a few. If you asked to have a candidate's sign on your lawn, it's yours. But always check local regulations first.

ADD ⟶ BALLOONS

GARAGE SALE ➡

NEW SIGN OVER SALVAGED POLITICAL SIGN

DETAILS

Weatherproof your sign by wrapping it in plastic or spritzing it with a waterproof spray. Most important, take it down after the sale.

SIGN SURFING

The website garagesalesource.com lets you create and print your own sign, though it's only the size of a piece of copy paper. At buildasign.com, you can design your own sign for just about any occasion in a variety of sizes and materials, and it can be created and delivered to you the next day.

Pick Fruit

Picking the right apple is tricky. Picking the right grapefruit is trickier. James Parker, a national produce buyer for Whole Foods, rides to the rescue with a bushel of helpful hints.

DEGREE OF DIFFICULTY: Easy. If you can follow a recipe, you can do this.

COST: You will save money by buying fruit you can actually eat.

IN GENERAL

Fruit is better when it's in season. You can check this guide at wholefoodsmarket.com/recipes/guides/fruits.php. When in doubt, ask your produce manager. In a hurry? A store will often promote the best fruit with a large and prominent display.

CITRUS

- For grapefruits and oranges, look for fruit that is relatively smooth. A more textured peel suggests a thicker rind and an immature fruit.

- Go for a relatively firm texture. A fruit that's too soft is probably overripe.

- Check the weight. If two fruits of the same variety and size have different weights, the heavier one is probably juicier. You can put a fruit in each hand to test which is heavier.

- Don't worry too much about color. A ripe grapefruit can be green. A ripe orange can be yellow or slightly green.

- As the peak domestic season (November-March) starts to wane in mid-March, you may want to start sizing down some of your citrus, for instance picking smaller navel oranges over the larger ones.

- Still confused? Pull out your trump card: "The best way to tell if you're making the right purchase decision is to sample it right there," Parker says. Ask a produce worker to cut you a piece.

APPLES

Look for firm fruit with no bruises or wrinkles.

PEARS

Look for firm fruit with no bruises or wrinkles. Buy a couple of days to a week before eating and leave the fruit out on the counter to ripen. Place near citrus to speed the ripening process.

BANANAS

Look for fruit with no visible bruises and store at room temperature. Fruit that's more green than yellow should keep 3-4 days.

Plant a Tree

Plant a tree? Sure! If Queen Elizabeth II is out there doing it in her mid-80s, you can too. Of course, HM has a retinue of staffers who do the heavy lifting: digging the hole, finding and positioning the tree, taking care of it afterward. She need only show up, brandish the royal spade, and ceremoniously flick a few scoops of impossibly well-groomed soil onto the spot.

For the rest of us, mere monarchs of a back 40 (be that inches, feet, acres or miles), the job of tree planting can be considerably more work unless we know what to do.

"There's a reason landscaping is a profession," said Sean Barry, a spokesman for the Arbor Day Foundation in Nebraska City,

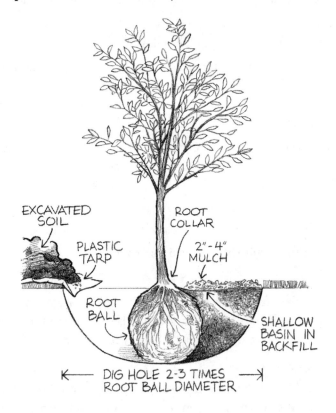

EXCAVATED SOIL

PLASTIC TARP

ROOT COLLAR

2"-4" MULCH

ROOT BALL

SHALLOW BASIN IN BACKFILL

|←—— DIG HOLE 2-3 TIMES ——→|
ROOT BALL DIAMETER

Neb. "It's possible to do it on one's own but there are a lot of steps and the possibility for a lot of mistakes."

Here are steps from the foundation for smart tree planting. Use them, if you like, on Earth Day, April 22. Note: Trees are sold in containers, with bare roots, or with the root ball wrapped in burlap; here is the foundation's advice on how to plant the latter. (Its website (arborday.org) offers information and videos on planting both types.)

DEGREE OF DIFFICULTY: Medium-low: Follow planting directions properly and you're all set.

WHAT YOU NEED: Shovel, work gloves, measuring tape or stick, tarp, wire cutters, utility knife, rake, garden hose, pruners. Optional: rototiller, wheelbarrow.

CHOOSING A TREE
You want the right tree in the right place on your property. Consider the height of the mature tree, how wide it will spread, what sort of shade it will provide. Will it drop fruit or make a mess of any sidewalk? Will it grow successfully in your climate? Talk it through with experts at your local cooperative extension service.

PREPARE THE SITE
Dig a saucer-shaped hole two or three times as wide but just as deep as the root ball, placing the soil on a tarp. (Rototilling an area five times the diameter and as deep as the root ball first will make hole digging easier.) The hole should have sloping sides; don't disturb the soil at the bottom of the hole.

PLANTING
Set the tree in the middle of the hole, handling the tree by the root ball and not the trunk. The tree's root collar, or flare, (where the roots meet the trunk) should be slightly above ground level; add some soil under the root ball, if necessary, to achieve proper

height. Cut away any wires, rope or twine from the root ball; remove any nails from the burlap. Pull the burlap back; cut off the loose material. You may leave regular burlap under the root ball; vinyl or treated burlap must be removed.

STANDING TALL

Is the tree standing straight? Stand back to make sure. Shovel the original soil around the root ball, packing it firmly to eliminate air pockets. Stop filling when the soil is level just below the root collar; rake the soil to create a shallow basin to hold water.

FINISHING TOUCHES

Water the tree well. Spread mulch 2 to 4 inches deep over the entire area of the filled hole, making sure the mulch is about 4 inches away from the trunk. Keep the mulch and soil around the tree moist but not soggy. Water every 7 to 10 days in dry weather during the tree's first year. Remove any tags or labels from the tree. Prune any broken or dead branches.

Polish Your Nails

STEP 1: PREP

CUT

You decide what's too long for you. The darker or bolder the polish, the shorter the nail.

FILE

Only in the direction the nail grows, so you don't weaken it. File sides straight, and corners round to match the cuticle's curve in reverse.

CLEAN

Use nail polish remover, whether there is polish to remove or not. It helps the future polish last longer. Really, it does.

STEP 2: THE CUTICLE

THE EASIEST WAY TO PUSH BACK THE CUTICLE: with a towel when you get out of the shower. You can also use a cuticle stick. NEVER: BITE YOUR CUTICLES. If you have itty bits of skin hanging around your nails, nip it off with a cuticle snipper.

STEP 3: THE BASE COAT

Always apply one. The ridge-filler that's part of the formula will smooth your nails and ready them for the color.

APPLICATION

Paint three fat stripes, first down the middle, then one on either side.

STEP 4: THE POLISH

Be sure to only dip your brush once per nail. If you double-dip for one nail, the polish might end up pooling.

FIRST COAT

Hold the flat side of brush parallel to your nail, don't come down from above—this is key to get the widest swath. Stroke the lacquer down the middle of the nail in a single sweep, then repeat on either side of the nail, again in single strokes. Do all 10 nails.

SECOND COAT

Make like you're swatting flies for a minute or two after the first coat, then repeat for second coat.

STEP 5: THE TOP COAT

Always. Always. Always. You might want to add a topper every two to three days, to keep your nails super glossy. If you type a lot, be sure to pull the top coat all the way over the tip.

STEP 6: DRYING TIME

PRODUCT

Quick-dry solution—drops or spray—usually dries nails within minutes.

AIR DRY

It'll take about an hour, and every object is a threat.

Smudge or nick? Put a little remover on your finger, and dab over the nick. Then go over that area again with color and top coat.

Repot a Houseplant

If you manage to keep alive a houseplant for, oh, more than a few months, there will surely come the day when it has outgrown its starter pot. The roots will be tangled. It will be gasping for air. It is especially wise to check in on your potted plants at winter's end (especially in certain climes), when the promise of vernal sun brings on hardy growth spurts, and your ready-to-burst houseplant begs for roomier real estate. (Some signs of a houseplant in need of roomier digs: It's top-heavy for the pot, or when roots start emerging from the existing pot's drainage holes.)

We checked in with Eric Larson, a houseplant wunderkind and manager of Yale University's Marsh Botanic Gardens in New Haven, Conn. He walked us through the not-so-slippery terrain of repotting your root-bound houseplant. Please, play along at home.

DEGREE OF DIFFICULTY: Easy.

WHAT YOU NEED: Old newspapers, clippers or pruning knife, potting soil (with vermiculite or perlite), new, clean pot that is no more than 25 percent bigger than existing pot, garden gloves.

STEP 1

Place old newspapers on a flat work space about the size of your kitchen sink. (If it's mild enough to do this outside, even better.) Gently remove your root-bound houseplant from its too-tight pot; this may require some light nudging.

STEP 2

Examine the root ball. Use a pruning knife or closed pruning clippers (your fingers will work, too) to gently tease out the roots, as if untangling a knot of hair—you are providing breathing room. Blackened roots indicate that the root is dead; cut it off. Be sure to do this on all sides of the root ball or the plant will be lopsided.

STEP 3

Slip your newly untangled/pruned houseplant into its new pot (no more than 25 percent bigger than the old one) to make sure you have at least 1 inch of headroom for every 8 inches of soil, so you can water without water spilling over the sides. Figure out how much potting soil you can tuck into the pot and still have adequate headroom. Now, take the houseplant back out of the new pot.

STEP 4

Add potting soil to the bottom of pot. Slip the plant back into its new home, filling in the sides with as much potting soil as you need. Tamp down the soil, and the plant. Water well to get rid of air pockets. Add additional soil if necessary.

Sew a Button

Erin Bried knows what intimidates people. "I've talked to so many powerful men and women who say, 'Omigod, I don't know how to sew on a button.' And it's like: 'You run a company. Why are you intimidated by this? The idea of bringing needle and

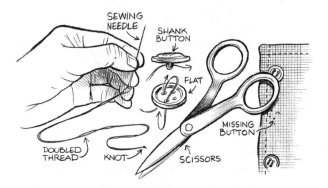

thread into anything is very intimidating for non-sewers," says the author of "How to Sew a Button: And Other Nifty Things Your Grandmother Knew" (Ballantine Books). Used to be for Bried too. Now? "I can sew a button on with the best of 'em," says the Self magazine senior editor, whose latest book is "How to Build a Fire: And Other Handy Things Your Grandfather Knew."

DEGREE OF DIFFICULTY: Easy

WHAT YOU NEED: Button, 1 to 5 minutes (or less), sewing needle, 2 feet of thread (max), scissors.

Here are Bried's tips for attaching these fasteners to your clothes.

TYPES: Flat (has holes through which one passes a thread-ed needle). Shank (has a protrusion with a hole on its underside).

CHOOSE: Similar size, style and shape to the former; it should slip easily (not loosely) through buttonhole.

STEP 1
Slip one end of thread through hole in needle, pull to meet other end. Knot; trim any excess thread.

STEP 2
Locate button's former position on clothing. See bits of thread? Tiny holes? That's it.

STEP 3
At button's former spot, push needle into fabric's backside; pull thread through. Slide button onto needle and down thread.

STEP 4
With button in place, push needle down through opposite hole (diagonally or adjacent—match sewing to other buttons on clothing) and out back of fabric. Push needle up from back of fabric to front through another hole. Repeat about four times, pulling thread tight. It's a four-hole button? Repeat with re-maining hole pair.

STEP 5
Push needle up through back of fabric to front—but not through holes in button. Wrap thread tightly around thread be-tween button and fabric several times to make a "shank"; thread needle through "shank" several times; snip thread. Done.

TIPS

- For quick repairs, prep several needles. Choose basic colors (white, black, gray, navy, brown). Use 20 to 24 inches of thread each. Thread each needle; knot ends. Poke needle point into pincushion (bar of soap, wine cork) to store.

- Button fall off? Check inside garment for a spare.

- Don't have a spare button and you're headed to a big meeting? "Pop off a button from a less conspicuous area—the bottom of your shirt, an extra one on your cuff," says Bried. "Use it to replace one that's more important."

Shine Leather Shoes

We got some tips from a pro, Michael Williams, who has shined shoes for "25 or 30" of his 74 years, he says, first on a French Quarter street corner in New Orleans and now at a stand in the lobby of the Roosevelt Hotel there.

DEGREE OF DIFFICULTY: If you can pick up a spilled drink, you can do this.

WHAT YOU NEED: Shoe brush, shoe polish that matches your shoe color (one with wax, not acrylic additives and no liquids), cotton rag, small can of lighter fluid

SUEDE SHOES

Get a special suede brush; if the shoe is only lightly dirty, rub chalk on it and remove it with a stiff brush. Be careful of solvents. "They can burn the shoe," he says.

STEP 1: CLEAN YOUR SHOES

A little spritz of water and a cloth will remove light dust and dirt.

FOR HEAVY DEPOSITS

Use a special shoe brush that has an edge for removing serious dirt.

DRY: Make sure the shoe is totally dry before polishing.

STEP 2: RESTORE THE TOE IF IT'S WORN

Sometimes a toe will have lost its color. Before polishing, take a tiny bit of lighter fluid on a rag and rub the toe down. Rub it very gently, let it dry, then polish.

STEP 3: APPLY POLISH

HOLDING THE SHOE

Put the shoe on your hand for better control.

APPLY

Use a stiff brush and a circular motion to rub the polish in, then use a softer brush to bring out the shine, shining with a back-and-forth motion using short strokes. Do the sides and back as well.

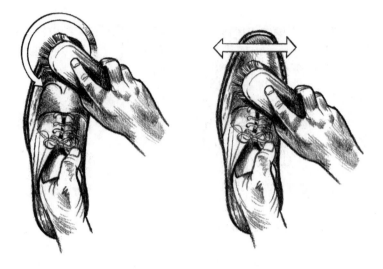

STEP 4: BUFF

Let the polish dry for five or 10 minutes, then buff to a shine, using a cotton cloth. Depending on use and weather, a shoe can hold a shine from three days to two or three weeks.

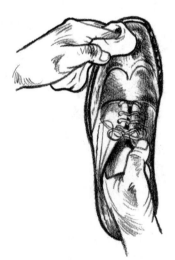

Snuff a Kitchen Fire

Let's hope you never need to do this. But just in case, here's what you need to know.

DEGREE OF DIFFICULTY: Medium: Actions are not difficult but required in a time of panic

WHAT YOU NEED: Pan lid, fire extinguisher, common sense

According to the National Fire Protection Association, four out of five fire-related deaths among civilians occur in the home. It makes sense to be prepared. Smoke alarms can alert you to a fire, and sprinklers can extinguish a blaze. Beyond that, fire extinguishers are a must, but even that might not be sufficient. If it's small enough and you think you can put it out, "always make sure everyone is out of the house and at a safe distance," says Heather Paul of State Farm Insurance.

KITCHEN FIRES

Most home fires occur in the kitchen; unattended cooking is the leading cause. For any kitchen fire, the first thing to do is turn off the heat. For a grease fire or any pan fire on the stove, place a metal lid or plate over the fire to cut off the oxygen supply. (And keep the lid on; lifting it resupplies oxygen and contents will burst back into flame).

Multi-purpose fire extinquisher: Aim at base of fire.

A fire extinguisher can handle a grease fire (don't use water; that only makes the fire spread). If the fire is contained to the pot, bank the spray from the extinguisher off the back of the stove or the bottom of the microwave if it's above the stove. If the oil or grease has already spilled and the top of the oven is on fire, sweep the spray of the extinguisher at the base of the fire. For a toaster fire, unplug the toaster and use an extinguisher. If a fire is in the oven or microwave, leave the door closed until the fire burns out.

Fire extinguishers are not created equal. Some are rated for fires involving paper, trash and cloth; some for fires involving flammable liquids; still others for electric fires. Some are multi-purpose, the best choice for homes.

Pan lid:
If safe to do so, put lid onto pan.

Oven fire:
Leave door closed until fire is out.

Burner control knob:
Turn off heat.

Not sure what to buy? Go to your local fire department or the NFPA website (nfpa.org).

Have an extinguisher on each floor of the home, but at least have one in the kitchen.

Familiarize yourself and your family with how the extinguisher works. (In general: Pull the pin, aim at the base of the fire, squeeze the trigger evenly, spray in a back-and-forth motion.) Check it annually to be sure it's filled and working properly. (The best place to have it looked over is at a fire station, Paul says.)

FIREFIGHTING STRATEGIES

If the room begins to fill with smoke, get out and call 911.

When fighting a fire, keep yourself between it and an exit, in case it gets out of control.

If a fire spreads or builds, get everyone out of the house and call the fire department. Kitchen fires can double in size every 60 seconds; speed is essential.

Never turn your back on a fire, even after it's out. Fires can rekindle almost instantly. Even if you extinguish it, call the fire department to make sure it is indeed out.

Tie a Bow Tie

A self-tied bow tie is to a clip-on as shoelace sneakers are to Velcro ones, says Richard Cristodero, neckwear buyer for Brooks Brothers. "No one over, like, 12 should be wearing a clip-on bow tie," he says. Men are wearing bow ties, he says; Brooks Brothers' bow tie sales are up 32 percent so far this year compared with the same period last year.

DEGREE OF DIFFICULTY: If you can tie a regular tie, you can master this.

TIME COMMITMENT: Thirty minutes to master the technique; under a minute once you do.

ASKING FOR HELP: OK only if you're under age 12 or the person you're smitten with volunteers

GET THEM HERE: epauletshop.com, beautiesltd.com, brooks-brothers.com

OR MAKE YOUR OWN: The process takes about 45 minutes. Visit tinyurl.com/yf2xu4n

STEP 1
Put tie around your collar. In your left hand, hold one end 1½ inches below the other end in your right hand.

STEP 2
Cross longer end over shorter end, and pass up through loop.

STEP 3
Form front loop of bow by doubling up the shorter end (hanging) and holding it horizontally.

STEP 4
Hold the front loop between the thumb and index finger of left hand. Drop long end down over front.

STEPS 5 AND 6
Place right index finger pointing up on bottom half of hanging part. Pass up behind front loop. Nudge resulting loop through knot behind front loop. Hold the bow at both folded ends and pull carefully to tighten the knot.

Wash a Dog

Your dog smells like a pair of sweat socks that have been dunked in cabbage soup. Little Spanky needs a bath, now. Forget the pricey groomer and tackle this one yourself. It will be quicker and cheaper and can be a bonding experience for the two of you.

STEP 1: THE WARM-UP

Brush and comb the dog thoroughly, eliminating all mats and tangles.

Inspect your pet for lumps, rashes, sores or injuries. If anything is suspicious, make a vet appointment.

STEP 2: THE MAIN EVENT

- **CLOSE THE DOOR:** When using the bathtub, remember to close the bathroom door so Spanky isn't tempted to make a break for it.

- **WET THE DOG:** Use a gentle stream of warm, not hot water. Use a plastic cup if you don't have a detachable shower head.

- **SHAMPOO:** Start at the neck and head on back. Massage gently into the coat, keeping the suds away from your pet's face; instead, use a wet washcloth and rub her face and head thoroughly.

- **RINSE:** Shampoo residue can make a dog itchy, so rinse twice.

- **BEWARE THE EARS:** No water in the ears. To clean, use a specially made ear-cleaning product. Soak a cotton ball, squeeze out the excess, and rub it around in the ear for a thorough cleaning.

STEP 3: THE COOL-DOWN

- **TOWELS:** Cover Spanky with a towel and lift her from the tub. Leave the towel in place for the inevitable violent shake/water show, then rub her down with more towels.

- **HAIR DRYER:** If your pet will tolerate it, use the hair dryer, set on low, to speed the drying process.

Comb little Spanky out again, and you're done.

Wash a Window

Few things give a homeowner as much satisfaction as clean windows—and we mean sparkling clean, I-never-knew-it-got-that-bright-outside clean. An afternoon of washing windows is time well spent. So grab a bucket, and let us begin an assault on grime.

DEGREE OF DIFFICULTY: Medium

WHAT YOU NEED: Bucket, cleaning solution, brush and/or sponge or rag, spray bottle, newspapers, squeegee, ladder(s).

THE GAME PLAN

Windows should be done on the inside and outside; start with the latter. If you run out of steam halfway through the project, you'll feel better if it's the more difficult outside part of the job that is finished first. Arm yourself with your tools and a cleaning solution, store-bought or make your own: one recipe is a solution of white vinegar and water, about 50-50 ratio, with a dash of dish soap.

WASHING INTERIOR GLASS

REMOVE CURTAINS AND BLINDS BEFORE WASHING GLASS

GET STARTED

Use a stepladder for easily reachable windows, an extension ladder for the second or third floors. Anything higher, find a professional. If using an extension ladder, call in a lackey to hold the ladder and pass you supplies (and run for coffee, come to think of it). Before you start slathering, check windows for cracks, chips or areas of missing putty. Repair as needed.

WASHING EXTERIOR WINDOWS

SQUEEGEE

TECHNIQUES

Outside, the windows will be dirtier; use a bucket and brush or sponge. Start at the top of the window and work your way down, washing with a steady circular motion. Wet the squeegee before starting. Make your first swipe horizontally at the very top, then make subsequent swipes vertically, top to bottom, wiping the squeegee between swipes. Finish off with a horizontal swipe across the bottom. Repeat if necessary.

Inside, remove clutter (window shades, blinds, curtains, etc.). Wipe windowsills with a damp cloth to remove dust and debris. Starting from top, spray cleaning solution on window or apply with a clean cloth. Wipe down glass to remove dirt. Squeegee or dry with newspaper (black and white; not colored ink), which won't leave streaks or lint like paper towels.

TIPS

- Don't clean windows in direct sunlight: It heats the glass and promotes streaks.

- A 12-inch squeegee is a good size; an 18-incher covers a lot more territory but can be unwieldy. If you have divided light windows with multiple panes, you need a small squeegee to fit inside the grilles. Measure the window before you buy.

SPRAY BOTTLE

OLD NEWSPRINT

- General squeegee nuggets: Make sure the blade is wet when you start; if you stop in the middle of a swipe, you'll leave a line; go edge to edge when you squeegee to avoid leaving a line.

Wash a Wine Glass

So you had friends over for wine and conversation. There was an Italian barolo, a California chardonnay, an albarino from Spain plus Neapolitan-style pizzas from a new place in town.

And now? Your friends have split and you have a dozen wine glasses, greasy plates, forks and a problem.

Stick everything in the dishwasher, invoke Bacchus and hope the stemware survives? Pile the glasses and greasy dishes in the sink, squirt in dishwashing soap, add water and scrub?

Or do what pros suggest: Use hot water and wash the wine glasses by hand.

So says Ray Foley, author of "Bartending for Dummies" (Wiley), founder of Bartender Magazine and a guy with 16 years tending bar under his belt. Sure, restaurants may run wine glasses through dishwashers, but hot water—just hot water, no soap—is the way to go, he says.

"Putting them in the dishwasher is not a bad thing, but...the problem with dishwashers and wine glasses is that, first, you can't find a dishwasher where they fit in," Foley says. "If they do fit, they clang against each other and some break." Plus, dishwasher rinses may leave a residue.

Foley walked us through the process.

DEGREE OF DIFFICULTY: Expect to spend 15 to 30 seconds per glass.

WHAT YOU NEED: Paper towels, dishcloth, hot water, cold water, drainer, rubber gloves optional.

STEP 1

Handle glasses one at a time. First, check the rim. "Lipstick is the biggest problem," Foley says, but there might be smudges from lips that have just eaten greasy foods. Wipe the wine glass around the rim with a paper towel.

STEP 2

Wash the glass in hot water, as hot as you can handle; wearing rubber gloves will allow you to use very hot water. If there was a lipstick stain or food smudge, re-wipe the rim with a paper towel.

STEP 3

Rinse well with cold water.

STEP 4

Set glass upside down on a drainer and allow to air dry. Don't use a cloth to dry glasses, Foley says: "You'll leave some lint on the glass."

STEP 5

Feel uneasy without soap? "If you want to, (use) just a pinch of the soap," Foley says, adding this cautionary note: "Then you've really got to rinse them really well in cold water and let them drain."

HEADS UP: Whether it's a mug or tall pilsner, bartending expert Ray Foley says, "never use soap with beer glasses. Sometimes it leaves a very light film so when you put the beer in, the beer will go flat."

Wrap a Gift

Need a system for wrapping rectangular boxes? Here's one of the best: simple, beautiful, even kind of eco. You'll save paper and ribbon with these directions from Wanda Wen, author of "The Art of Gift Wrapping: 50 Innovative Ideas Using Organic, Unique, and Uncommon Materials" (Potter Craft).

The cornerstone of her technique: accurately sized paper, eliminating the gaping and clumping that torment amateur wrappers. The flourish is a ribbon that looks clean and classic, yet goes on without an inch of waste and comes off with a single pull.

You wrap the box with ribbon without cutting it until you're done, ensuring "that you're not cutting a piece of ribbon that's too long or too short," Wen says, "because that's another pet peeve of people, especially if you're using expensive ribbon."

STEP 1

Put box down on the gift wrap. Cut a rectangle of paper large enough to comfortably wrap the present.

STEP 2

TRIM THE WIDTH OF THE PAPER: Place the rectangle of paper on the table; put the gift on top. Loosely wrap the paper around the box's width and depth and add 2 inches of overlap; trim.

STEP 3

TRIM THE LENGTH OF THE PAPER: Now place the box on the bottom edge of the rectangle of paper. Stand the box on its end and then push it down and away from you to measure out the length and depth. Again, factor in another 2 inches of overlap; trim.

STEP 4

Put box, bottom up, in the middle of the paper.

STEP 5

WRAP THE WIDTH: Bring one side of the paper up and, using double-stick tape, affix it to the box. Take the other edge of the paper, fold it in about ½ inch (to hide the raw edge), and affix it with the tape to the top of the box. The seam should be in the middle, with no raw edges and no visible tape.

STEP 6

FINISH ENDS: Press the paper in toward the box on both the left and the right, forming sharp diagonal creases on the top flap. Tape the top flap to the box. Now form the same sharp creases on the bottom end, but before taping this end to the box, fold in the raw edge about ½ inch to create a perfect edge. Tape to box.

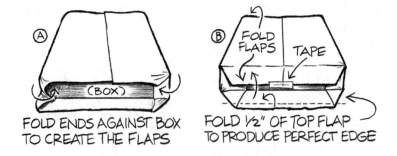

Ⓐ (BOX)
FOLD ENDS AGAINST BOX
TO CREATE THE FLAPS

Ⓑ FOLD FLAPS   TAPE
FOLD ½" OF TOP FLAP
TO PRODUCE PERFECT EDGE

STEP 7

Gently using your fingertips, create sharp creases along the edges of the box.

STEP 8

NOW THE BOW: Don't cut ribbon off the spool. Take the loose end and pull out a length sufficient for one of the bow loops and a tail—about 10 inches total. Take that 10-inch length and anchor it at the center of the box, with the loose end dangling off the left side.

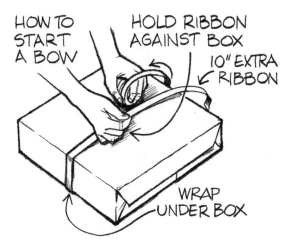

HOW TO START A BOW

HOLD RIBBON AGAINST BOX

10" EXTRA RIBBON

WRAP UNDER BOX

STEP 9

Holding the spool with your right hand on the right side of the box, and the 10-inch tail secured with your left hand, wrap the ribbon around the width of the box one time, come back to the center, and hold the ribbon with your left hand; now turn the spool end down toward the bottom of the box and wrap the length of the box.

STEP 10

Bring the spool end of the ribbon back to the middle of the box, and hold the ribbon with your left hand. Use your right hand to cut another 10-inch tail.

STEP 11

Bring the new tail down to the bottom left corner of the box and thread it back under the intersection of ribbons at the center. Tie a bow.

AT THE OFFICE

Ask for a Raise

Asking your boss for a raise, especially in a tough economy, takes preparation and finesse. Danny Huffman, co-founder and CEO of Career Services International, a career management firm headquartered in Orlando, Fla., gives pointers.

DEGREE OF DIFFICULTY: Probably easier to ask for a kidney.

WHAT YOU NEED: Courage, piece of paper, pen, compromising photos of your boss. Not really. This is bad form.

STEP 1

Keep a journal in which you make note of all contributions you make to the company that go above and beyond what you were hired to do. If you assisted in the creation of a spreadsheet that saved the company time or money, jot it down, because that is the kind of detail you might forget when the time comes to make your case for a raise.

STEP 2

MERIT NOT TENURE: "You don't deserve a raise because you've been in the same position for two years," Huffman said. "You deserve a raise if you've (helped) the bottom line."

STEP 3

MAKE A DATE: Casually saying you'd like to talk about money might put your boss on the defensive. Plus, this isn't casual. Make a date to talk about "how we can both continue to grow and expand."

STEP 4

PRESENT A WRITTEN PROPOSAL: Hand your boss a hard copy of a well-written proposal that lays out what your goals were when you were hired, what you've done to exceed them, and how you're going to continue to improve. Not only does it in-dicate that you're professional and care about the company, a document also can be entered in your permanent record, which might save you if the company has to downsize.

KNOW YOUR NUMBER: Be realistic and willing to negotiate. Generally, an hourly or entry-level worker might go for a 3 percent to 5 percent raise; middle management might ask for 7 percent to 8 percent; and executives might seek 10 percent to 15 percent.

AVOID DISCUSSING WHY: Employers want someone committed to the company, so it shouldn't matter that you're having a child or a parent is ill.

STEP 5

DON'T THREATEN TO QUIT: Employers need to feel that they are in control, so leveraging will come back and bite you later. However, if you have an offer from another company, it's courtesy to let your boss know, to give him/her a chance to fight to keep you.

STEP 6

REJECTION: If your boss turns you down, suggest that you'd like to develop a plan for yourself so that you can revisit the issue in three to six months. "Here's the dedication, here's the task at hand, here's what I'm going to do," Huffman said. "They will love that."

Clean a Computer Keyboard

Extend the life of your keyboard by keeping it clean.

Computer users sometimes are startled by the discovery of non-native species harbored by their keyboard. Dust bunnies, crumb colonies and Coke deposits can be safely relocated without the blast of an aerosol can, computer chip designer Karl Brummel assures us. Here are his tips.

DEGREE OF DIFFICULTY: Easy, if you do routine cleaning, and keep food and drink away from the keyboard—or you have expendable income to keep replacing it.

WHAT YOU NEED: Paper towels or newspaper, "canned air," spray cleaner. Optional: wet/dry vac.

REMOVE-AND-REPLACE METHOD

"I have considerable expertise in this area," Brummel says. His technique:

STEP 1

Buy a new keyboard.

STEP 2

Discard /recycle old keyboard.

Brummel hastens to mention that replacement keyboards cost as little as $9 unless they are on a laptop or otherwise built-in. Even then, he wouldn't rule out the remove-and-replace modality. "However, then you have to add a backup/restore phase in between steps 1 and 2."

If pressed to elaborate—or to salvage the keyboard and attached components—he endorses the following methodology.

ROUTINE KEYBOARD CLEANING

Regular light cleaning prevents overheating and extends the life of your machine. Keep food and beverages on a separate surface.

Spread newspaper or towel below computer. Turn keyboard upside down and shake gently to dislodge debris.

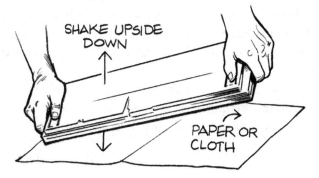

WHEN MORE IS REQUIRED: IF IT HAS BEEN A WHILE OR NEVER...AND YOU DON'T WANT TO BUY A NEW KEYBOARD:

STEP 1

Take keyboard outside. Spray "canned air" (sold at office supply and computer stores) at an angle between keys, in such a way as to drive debris up and out rather than deeper. Turn the keyboard over and gently shake any stubborn particles loose.

COMPRESSED AIR

STEP 2

Wipe a damp paper towel over keys and other surfaces. If a board is really grimy, use spray cleaner, such as Windex or Formula 409, on a paper towel. Dry with paper towel or lint-free cloth.

CAUTIONARY NOTE: "I wouldn't spray an aerosol on a keyboard," Brummel says. "On laptops the motherboard is basically right below the keyboard. But even regular detached keyboards have some circuitry under the keys, and it's not good to get it wet."

OPTIONAL AND AT YOUR OWN RISK: The obsessive may wish to run the dusting brush of the vacuum over the keyboard, but some technicians warn this can damage the electronics.

SPILLS

If that cup of coffee just spilled itself, try the following triage.

STEP 1

Turn off and unplug computer. If the spill is significant and a wet/dry vac is available, Brummel would use it immediately. Or tilt keyboard to side or turn upside-down to drain.

SPILL

DAMP CLOTH

STEP 2

Wipe surfaces with damp cloth.

STEP 2.5

Optional and at your own risk: Take photo of keyboard. Pry keyboard caps off with a flathead screwdriver. (Do not dislodge the large caps over the space, enter and shift keys.) "Prying off keys sometimes works, but about half the time you have to break them to get them off," Brummel says. In addition, doing so may violate your warranty, in which case you could have saved yourself a headache with the regimen in Part I. Gently clean innards of keys with a cotton swab dampened with water, or 90 percent isopropyl alcohol for stubborn gunk. Use "canned air" again, if desired.

STEP 3

Air-dry completely. Replace caps.

Clean Your Desk

Keeping your workspace clean is half elbow grease, half willpower. Here's how to get it done.

DEGREE OF DIFFICULTY: Hard. Why? Because stuff makes humans feel alive. If we can see lots of stuff, so much the better.

WHAT YOU NEED: Spray cleaner, paper towels and no heart.

Asking someone if they want a clean desk is like asking if they'd like to be fed chocolate ice cream by a model. "Um...wait...letme-thinkaboutthatyes!"

Yet the number of people who actually have clean desks is about as high as those model-fed fortunate ones. But getting (and keeping) a clean desk is easy. And clean doesn't mean organized. Clean means people walk past and wonder if someone works there. Clean means as little as possible, accompanied by next-to-godliness surfaces, and you want it. You know you do. People who say they "know where everything is" are delusional. No, they don't, unless they're looking for a mess.

HOW TO DO IT: Here's the secret to getting a clean desk, and keeping it that way: Nothing that you can hold in your hand is your friend. People print out e-mails. Why? Those copies of past reports, or congratulatory letters from your boss, you're keeping because ...? Out. Everything out. If you've ever watched professional packers prepare a house for a move, it's easy to understand. You have about 12 seconds to decide whether something is going, and what box it goes in. After that, they take over.

STEP 1: PILE IT UP. ALL OF IT.

Put everything in a big pile, then dump it in the trash. Now look at your desk with nothing on it. Nice, right? Now, do you really want to pick through the trash? So *honestly* decide what you need. My needs are: lamp, phone, computer and two pictures. Not three. Two. If you honestly evaluate your pile, you'll find that you *need* very little.

STEP 2: CLEAN. THOROUGHLY.

Squirt cleaner until your eyes water, and scrub. Now look again. What do you think about that pile now? Anything that threatens your desk's sanctity should be thrown away. You don't need paper, pens go in drawers and urgent matters get a file in a drawer, not atop your desk.

STEP 3: PRESERVE.

It will seem hard at first, to throw almost everything away. But you get used to it. And now you have time to find a model, with chocolate ice cream and a spoon.

DIY Facial Massage

A common plight of the "office athlete"—whose sport entails sitting for hours staring at a computer—is facial pain brought on by long bouts of reading, screen glare and teeth-grinding.

Left unchecked, facial pain can produce sinus and tension headaches, toothaches, blurred vision and the pressure-cooker feeling that your head might explode, said Cynthia Ribeiro, president-elect of the American Massage Therapy Association and an instructor at the National Holistic Institute, a massage school in California.

Happily, help is literally at your fingertips. At least once a week (ideally, once a day) give yourself a face massage to relieve the muscle tension, Ribeiro said. She shared some techniques for massaging key facial trigger points. Apply light to moderate pressure to avoid aggravating any issue. You should feel a "good" pain; if it hurts too much, back off.

FOR TEMPORAL HEADACHES

Press four fingers against the temporal muscle and move them back and forth, up and down or in a circular motion.

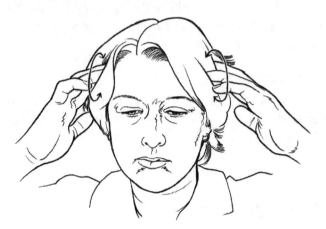

FOR FRONTAL AND SINUS HEADACHES

Put three fingers of each hand above the eyebrow line and press left to right, to the hairline, without gliding.

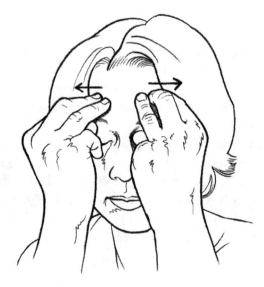

FOR TENSION HEADACHES, TIRED EYES AND SINUSES

Press your thumbs up against the underside of the brow bone in the eye socket.

FOR STRESS AND TENSION THROUGHOUT THE BODY

(If you have time for only one exercise, this is the one to do): Using your three middle fingers arranged in a triangle, apply pressure just above the bridge of your nose, known as the "third eye."

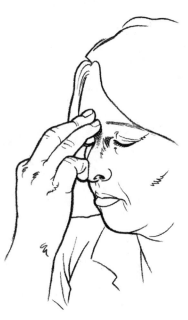

FOR SINUS HEADACHES AND ALLERGIES

With your index and middle fingers, press along, above and below your cheekbones.

Avoid Dog Bites

Although fatalities are rare, more than a half-million people a year, mostly children, require hospital treatment for dog bites, according to the American Veterinary Medical Association. And thousands were less serious and unreported. Clearly, people need to wise up.

"It's very important for parents to teach children how to behave around dogs without frightening them," says Dr. Pamela Reid, vice president of the Animal Behavior Center for the American Society for the Prevention of Cruelty to Animals. "Part of it is teaching the child appropriate behaviors around dogs, and also teaching the child what to look for, what to watch for, interpreting the body language. That's a little more difficult."

READING A DOG

Most dogs will give a warning signal, or signals, before biting. But they can be very subtle. Sometimes they're obvious, like a snarl, bared teeth and growl. Sometimes it's just a tenseness in the face or a sideways glance that indicates a dog is stressed. And a stressed dog can bite just like a vicious one.

WARNING / DANGER
SIGNALS

EARS BACK

TEETH BARED

Some indicators of trouble are a dog's eyes (larger- or smaller-than-normal eyes can indicate stress, excitement, fear or a feeling of being threatened); its mouth (a closed mouth may indicate stress; a dog's lips can telegraph its intentions); ears (erect, forward-pointing ears can mean a dog is being attentive or contemplating an attack, while ears back, flattened, may indicate fear or submissiveness); and tail (wagging doesn't always mean it is happy).

The ASPCA offers a lengthy lesson in dogs' body language, complete with helpful photographs, at aspca.org (type "canine body language" in the search field).

THINGS TO REMEMBER:

- Avoid making eye contact with a dog, and never disturb a dog that's sleeping, eating or that has puppies. Don't pet a dog unless it sniffs you first; present a closed hand, and let the dog check you out. When you do pet it, gently rub the shoulder or chest, not the top of the head.

PETTING A DOG AVOID TOP OF DOG'S HEAD ↘

TYPICALLY SAFER LOCATIONS ↘

- If approached by a strange dog, stand still and let it sniff you. When the dog is satisfied and loses interest, slowly walk away—don't run or scream. If the dog is aggressive and begins chasing you, put something between you and the dog—a backpack or a jacket, for example. Let the dog have it while you carefully escape.

- Children should never approach a strange dog or play with any dog unless an adult is present. If knocked over by a dog, a child should pull himself into a ball and remain motionless.

IF YOU'RE BITTEN

Wash a wound with soap and water. If it's a serious bite, get medical attention. Report the incident to animal control. Don't try to catch the dog. Because the vast majority of victims are bitten by dogs they know, dogs are usually easy to track down. If it is a strange dog, call in the report immediately. (Report any strange dog roaming in a neighborhood before they have a chance to bite somebody.)

Babysit a 1-Year-Old

Watch your pal's kid for the afternoon? Sure! How hard could it be? Do it well, and your pal will be eternally grateful. (But don't do it too well, or your pal will come knocking every Saturday.)

DEGREE OF DIFFICULTY: Can you handle china dishes? You're golden.

WHAT YOU NEED: Snacks, diapers, hand sanitizer, cell numbers for all parents

STEP 1: FEED IT

If you're spending more than 15 minutes together, the child will need to eat. Don't worry, strained peas are a thing of the past. By age 1, "your toddler can eat just about anything you do, with the exception of choking hazards," according to our favorite eating manual, "Super Baby Food" by Ruth Yaron. But don't be the joker who gives a toddler Doritos. Better bets: avocado, banana, graham crackers, a bagel, cooked pasta. Ask the parents about allergies and keep pieces to the size of a Cheerio (also a good snack).

STEP 2: CHANGE IT

You will not avoid diaper duty, so embrace it early and often. The parents will likely leave supplies: diapers, wipes, diaper cream. Should you run out of diapers, try this tip from "Be Prepared: A Practical Handbook for New Dads" by Gary Greenberg: 1. Lay out a dish towel and place an athletic sock in the center, lengthwise. 2. Fold over the sides of the dish towel to make a square. 3. Lay the child on top of the towel and fold the bottom part between his legs so it rests on top of his midsection. 4. Tuck the front corners inside the back corners and secure with duct tape, making sure duct tape doesn't touch skin.

STEP 3: TRANSPORT IT

If your home features sharp corners, breakable objects or a pet, you're best served to do the baby-sitting off-site. If you must drive, know that the car seat belongs in the back—always—and can face forward now that the child is age 1 or older. Secure all buckles and make sure nothing is within arm's reach of the seat—especially yesterday's dry-cleaning pickup. Plastic bags + small children = disaster. If possible, opt for public transportation. Toddlers adore trains and buses.

STEP 4: ENTERTAIN IT

Aquariums are loud, colorful and relatively toddler-proof (the important stuff's all protected by shatterproof glass). Plus, "aquariums provide people with valuable information about the importance of oceans, waters, and the animals that live there... and can inspire conservation action," according to a 2005 Harris Interactive poll. If you don't live near an aquarium, the live fish display at a Bass Pro Shops or Cabela's will do in a pinch.

STEP 5: RETURN IT

Take a bow. You fed, changed and wore out a toddler. Now it's nap time—for both of you. Oh, and tell the parents to keep your dish towel.

Bowl Without Hurting Anyone

After one too many gutter balls, it's time to take a hard look at your bowling skills—or lack thereof. Bob Rea, lead instructor at Ithaca, N.Y.-based Dick Ritger Bowling Camps, which holds sessions nationwide, breaks down the basics of bowling technique. Note: The steps below are for right-handed bowlers; left-handed bowlers should reverse the directives.

DEGREE OF DIFFICULTY: Medium

WHAT YOU NEED: Bowling ball, bowling shoes

PICK THE RIGHT BALL

Generally, a ball should be 10 percent of body weight (up to 16 pounds). To ensure proper fit, insert your thumb and lay your middle and ring fingers flat over the ball. The crease of your mid-finger knuckles should be centered over their respective holes.

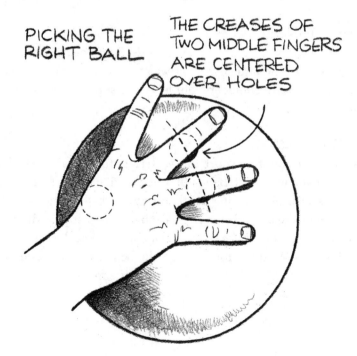

PICKING THE RIGHT BALL

THE CREASES OF TWO MIDDLE FINGERS ARE CENTERED OVER HOLES

FIND YOUR STARTING POSITION

Go up to the foul line, turn and take four and a half normal strides toward the seats. That's where to start. Stand on or near the center dot on the floor, also known as the approach. Then find the target: Rather than aim for the pins, focus on the lane arrows (the first set is about 12 feet up the alley); aim for the second arrow in from the right.

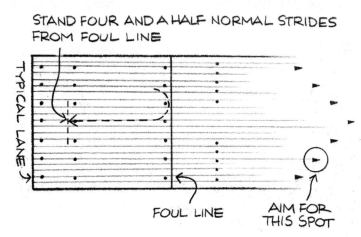

STAND FOUR AND A HALF NORMAL STRIDES FROM FOUL LINE

TYPICAL LANE

FOUL LINE

AIM FOR THIS SPOT

THE STANCE

Stagger feet so left heel is even with right toe. Bend knees slightly, lean forward slightly at waist. Hold ball at waist level, in line with right shoulder; your left hand supports most of the ball's weight.

THE APPROACH

As you take your first short step with right foot, push the ball in front of you with both hands (like you're giving it to someone). Release your nonbowling hand, letting the ball swing back. At the end of the second step the ball should be just past the bottom of the swing; at the third step it should be at the top of the back swing. With the fourth step, the ball swings forward and your left foot slides to a smooth stop at the foul line.

RELEASE

Imagine a clock face-up on the foul line, with 12 o'clock facing the pins. Your middle and ring fingers should be at 4 and 5 o'clock when the ball rolls off your fingers.

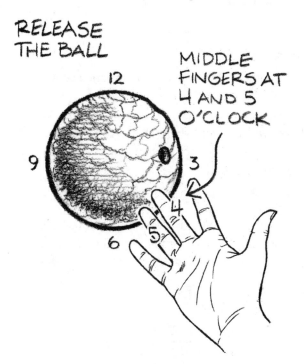

RELEASE
THE BALL

MIDDLE
FINGERS AT
4 AND 5
O'CLOCK

12

9   3

6

NAIL THE FINISH

Once the ball is gone, maintain the knee bend and slight forward lean at the waist, with your left arm outstretched to the side for balance. Your trailing leg should end crossed behind you, slightly left of your spine. Continue swinging your right arm forward, then scoop your hand back as though you're answering a phone, ending with your hand slightly above your head.

Grab a Cab

There's a right way and a wrong way to flag a taxi—just ask the experts, aka the drivers.

DEGREE OF DIFFICULTY: Easy.

WHAT YOU NEED: A firm wave (smartphone is optional).

Taking a cab might not seem to be that complicated. But as any taxi driver will tell you, there are ways to do it safely, quickly and cleanly—and ways not to. So from the experts, we give you some tips for the road.

THE HAIL
Alfred LaGasse, CEO of the Taxicab, Limousine & Paratransit Association, says that there are actually two parts to the successful hailing of a taxicab.

THE GESTURE

Make a sign that's recognizable by the driver. It should be easily viewable from a distance so the taxi has ample room to move to the curb. "Be clear with the signal," LaGasse said. "Don't be half-hearted about it." Put your hand up and out, like you are waving to someone. A casual, half-raised arm might not get anyone's attention.

GET IN POSITION

Put yourself in a safe place for the cab to stop. "Be cognizant of your surroundings, and be sure he can stop," he said. Stand at least 30 feet away from the corner, as you don't want to ever enter or exit a cab in the middle of an intersection. And always, ALWAYS, hail from the curb. Never hail from the street. "Don't put your driver in a bad position," LaGasse warned.

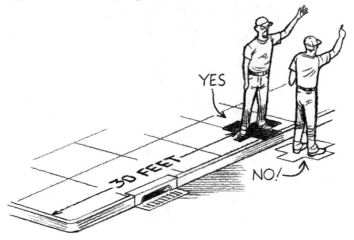

YES

30 FEET

NO!

TIPPING

Cabs are in a service industry, and drivers—like most service workers—depend on gratuities for income. LaGasse suggested thinking of it as you would a server at a restaurant: 15 percent for expected service, up to 20 percent for a great experience and down to 10 for something less than wonderful. Add $1 per bag that the cabbie helps you with and $2 per bag for any that are very heavy.

HAVE DIRECTIONS READY

You've hired a taxi, not a field guide. Although many taxi drivers will be familiar with all parts of an area they serve, inevitably there will be gaps in a cabbie's knowledge. Try to know the major streets of your route or a landmark that the driver will know near your destination.

THERE'S AN APP FOR THAT

What if you're in a place without a significant number of cabs looking for a fare? Or, horrors, you're in a place that doesn't allow people to hail from the sidewalk? If you have a smart phone (think iPhone, Android or BlackBerry), apps such as Taxi Magic will bring a cab to you in many markets.

SMART
PHONE
TAXI APP

DO UNTO OTHERS

LaGasse asked a favor of passengers: Be kind to the taxi even if someone else hasn't. If you get in a clean cab, it's because the passenger before you left it clean. "Treat the vehicle with respect, because that vehicle is going to go out and serve someone else," he said.

Keep Score at the Ballpark

People have been keeping scorecards at baseball games since before players wore gloves, but the popularity of keeping a scorecard seems to have faded in recent decades.

James L. Gates Jr., library director at the National Baseball Hall of Fame and Museum and a scorekeeper on the Little League, American Legion, college and minor-league levels, says he views a baseball scorecard "as a first draft of history" and considers each one a work of art.

So let's take a brief look at how to score a game. These are just the basics, a more or less traditional method of keeping score. There are modernized versions (reisnerscorekeeping.com/how), but for our purposes, we'll keep score the old-fashioned way. Grab a beer and some peanuts and let's get started.

THE WARM-UP

There will be a scorecard in the program you buy at the ballpark, or you can go online and print your own (baseballscorecard.com is one of many sites offering downloads).

The scorecard is a grid (you need one for each team). Down the left side is space for a player's uniform number, name and position. The rest of the scorecard is a block of individual squares in which plays are noted (each has a diamond in it, representing the field). By reading across, you can see what a player did in his day's work. Each vertical column is an inning, and by reading down a column you can see what both teams did offensively and defensively during that inning.

TALKING BASEBALL

Each position on the field is assigned a number. A pitcher is 1, catcher 2, first baseman 3, etc. Plays made on the field also have their own shorthand: A strikeout is K. The letter is written backward if a batter is called out on strikes. (See chart for a longer list.)

PLAY BALL

Remember, no gaps; every play needs to be recorded to have a record of the game.

Start by filling in the starting lineups: the players, their uniform number, their position number.

Now watch the game. Let's say the first batter, Burnson, is called out on strikes. Put a backward K in the middle of the diamond and a circled 1 (for the first out) in the lower left portion of Burnson's first-inning box. Next up: Friedmann. He hits a grounder to the third baseman (5) who throws to the first baseman (3) for the out. So put 5-3 in the diamond and a circled 2 in the lower left part of the box next to Friedmann's name. Next up is Zabicki, who hits a double. In the little diamond in Zabicki's first-inning box, darken the line from home to second base, indicating a double.

The key is to track a player's progress in each at-bat. So if there is a wild pitch that moves Zabicki from second to third, write WP (for wild pitch) in the box and darken his base path line to third. The fourth batter of the inning, McFadden, flies out to left field: Write F7 (flyout to left fielder) in the diamond and put a circled 3 in his first-inning box.

As plays get more complicated, so does the scoring. A third-to-second-to-first double play is 5-4-3, and the runner who was forced at second gets a darkened line drawn only halfway to second base, indicating he never reached it. At the point that darkened line stops, write the uniform number of the player who hit into the double play. If his force at second was the first out of the inning, he'd get a circled 1 in his box (second out, a circled 2); the batter who hit into the double play would get 5-4-3 written across his diamond, and a circled 2 (or 3) to denote the number of outs.

TIPS

- If a player scores a run, the entire diamond is blackened in.
- When a player is replaced, write his substitution below his name.
- Depending on the scorecard you use, there may be two rows of small boxes (one for strikes, one for balls) within the player's box to keep track of the count. Other scorecards have room for attendance, weather, weather conditions, etc.
- At the end of each half-inning, draw a heavy line across the bottom of the box of the last player to bat. Next inning, start one column to the right with the next batter up.

CUSTOMIZE IT

Once you get the basic system down, embellish as you see fit. Use the basic abbreviations or devise your own. Just as no two baseball games are identical, no two scorecards—even for the same game—will be identical.

TAKING IT TO THE NEXT LEVEL

Two websites that can offer additional information are base-ballscorecard.com and baseball.about.com (type "keeping a scorecard" in the search field). These also include tutorials to help you further refine your skill.

POSITIONS

1: pitcher 2: catcher 3: first baseman 4: second baseman 5: third baseman 6: shortstop 7: left fielder 8: center fielder 9: right fielder dh: designated hitter

Some common abbreviations used in scoring

- 1B: single
- 2B: double
- 3B: triple
- A: assist
- AB: at-bat
- B: bunt
- BB: base on balls (walk)
- BK: balk
- CS: caught stealing
- DP: double play
- E: error
- F: flyout
- FC: fielder's choice
- FO: foul out or force out
- GDP/GIDP: grounded into double play
- GRD: ground-rule double
- HBP: hit by pitch
- HR: home run
- K: strikeout
- LOB: left on base
- OBS: obstruction
- PB: passed ball
- PH: pinch hitter
- PO: putout
- R: run
- RBI: run batted in
- SAC: sacrifice
- SB: stolen base
- SF: sacrifice fly
- U: unassisted putout
- WP: wild pitch

Make Outfield Grass Patterns at Home

You've no doubt sat in the stands of your favorite baseball stadium, admired that meticulously lined outfield grass and thought, "Wow, my lawn would look great like that!" Well no problem, slugger. Step right up to the plate and take a swing at these tips from Major League Baseball's most legendary groundskeeper, Roger Bossard of the Chicago White Sox, who is in his 44th season with the team and consults for 14 other teams, plus four football teams.

DEGREE OF DIFFICULTY: Like dragging a kid on a sled for quite some time.

STEP 1: THE GREENEST GRASS

NUTRIENTS
To get the proper contrast, you need a thick, green lawn. Instead of the standard four applications of lawn nutrients, Bossard suggests six or seven, to darken the grass for "a better striping effect."

CUT THE LAWN
Any length, any direction.

BUST OUT YOUR ROLLER
Lawn flatteners can be attached to your mower or pushed by hand. They start at $100. Try Home Depot or Lowe's.

STEP 2: START TO ROLL

BEGIN AT AN EDGE
Trail the flattener behind you as you walk a straight line across the lawn. Bossard begins at second base and rides straight to the warning track in center field. Because this is the most important step, Bossard ties a string from his start point to his end point to guide him. "The truth of the fact is you're basing your whole system on the first line. If you screw up one line, the whole thing is screwed up. That's why the night before, I don't allow a mower to drink."

TURN AROUND
Go back against the line you've already made but in the other direction, going over the edge of the first line by two or three inches. Repeat until the lawn is done.

STEP 3: THE COVETED CHECKERBOARD
After going vertical, go horizontal, following the exact same procedure. Again, the first line is crucial. Going over what you've already done won't harm your previous good work. "Believe it or not, when you do the pattern over and over, it doesn't undo what you've done."

Pack for Road Trips

TRAVELING BAGS

COOLER

WATER BOTTLES →

DEGREE OF DIFFICULTY: Easy. Hitting the road with the family is a summer tradition. Here are packing tips to make that trip smoother.

WHAT YOU NEED: A vehicle, cooler, traveling bags—and an ability to embrace minimalism.

THE PRELIMINARIES

First things first: Get your vehicle travel-ready, says Salwa Jabado, associate editor at Fodor's Travel.

"Get a tuneup, get an oil change, check things like the wipers," she says. "And get AAA. If you lock your keys in the car, it makes things so much easier."

Also, clean out the car. Unload the junk in your trunk and leave it at home.

CHOOSE SMARTLY

"The biggest mistake people make is taking too much," says Erin Bried, who devotes a section of her book, "How to Build a Fire and Other Handy Things Your Grandfather Knew" (Ballantine Books, $15), to prepping for a car trip. "You're going on a road trip to explore, to see the world. Why take 14 pairs of shoes?"

"People pack like they're going on an airplane trip," Jabado adds. "Rather than one huge, indestructible piece of luggage that fills the trunk, pack smaller duffel bags (for) each passenger."

Jabado also suggests packing baby wipes, paper towels and a roll of toilet paper "in case you have to make a stop at some gas station." Also pack bags for trash, resealable plastic bags for wet swimsuits, sweaters (that air conditioning can get cold), pillows, blankets and things to entertain the kids. Have a first-aid kit handy (it should be easily accessible).

Bring a crushable cooler, not that giant gonzo thing you use on the Fourth of July. Fill it with water, juice and healthy snacks.

THE LOADING

Take only what you need. Bried suggests that before you start loading the car, set out all your stuff—"then put half of it back." Place what makes the cut in a number of small bags, then take it all outside and set it by the car. You'll get some visual perspective and a nice overview of the packing job ahead.

"I think it's a good idea to have one person handle the packing," Bried suggests. "Others can carry things out, but have just one person packing."

Put the biggest item in first, and place the little packages around it—"work the angles," as Bried says. Take your time; think of this as a sort of jigsaw puzzle.

If you can lock your vehicle in your garage or another secure location overnight, pack the night before. If you wait till the morning of your trip, you might rush things and get careless.

Avoid loading up your roof. It can make the vehicle top-heavy and unstable.

"Unless you're going for a really long time, you should be able to pack efficiently enough to fit it all in the car," Bried says. "This sounds a little wonky, but gas prices are going up, and the more you tie to the top of the car, the more gas you're going to use. Everything you pack will cost you a little more money."

Photograph a Dog

When photographer James Morrissey schedules a portrait setting for a dog, he blocks out three hours.

"It's not (getting the subject used to) the equipment, it's me, getting them used to me," says Morrissey, owner of Wild Coyote Studio (wildcoyotestudio.com) in New York. "You don't want to be the exciting new thing, so to speak."

So there's one advantage you have when photographing your pet: Your dog knows you, making it easier to get his personality to come through.

Morrissey, who was the green room photographer at this year's Westminster Kennel Club dog show and who offers a free forum at nwpphotoforum.com, is happy to share his dog photography expertise.

DEGREE OF DIFFICULTY: Practice makes perfect. And hey, it's your dog. This is fun!

WHAT YOU NEED: Camera (SLR preferred); props and/or squeak toys, optional.

EQUIPMENT

He doesn't recommend a brand, but does recommend a style: "The best type of camera for pet photography is probably still the SLR (single lens reflex)," he says. "Even the cheapest ones offer a lot of control and snappy auto focus." If money is tight, consider purchasing a used digital SLR and some third-party lenses. "Digital cameras depreciate quickly, so used bodies may be a very affordable alternative."

PROPS

It depends on the dog, he says. Some respond, some don't. He has very few props in his photos. "Props can be very powerful. I don't use them frequently. I think you need to be very sparing."

He adds that photography is the opposite of painting. "When you're painting you're building a canvas that starts with nothing. Photography is all about reduction. You want to clean up your background, focus on your subject. Whenever you clutter things up it gets harder when it comes to creating a beautiful composition."

ATTENTION-GRABBERS

"You should see my arsenal. Turkey calls, duck calls, squeak toys. That's the fun part of the game, all the toys." Morrissey finds this especially helpful when photographing two or more dogs. It doesn't have to be that complicated, he says. A crinkling empty potato chip bag or empty plastic water bottle can grab their attention. He tries to avoid using treats. "I will if I have to. Some dogs are just treat motivated. But I try not to. It creates saliva, and a ruly dog sometimes will become unruly if they're just fixated on a treat."

PET PREP

Bathing and grooming are always a positive. "You want to photograph dogs when they look their best. After they've been to the groomer, been bathed, that's a wonderful time to photograph a dog. And before they go in the backyard and get muddied up."

LIGHTING

"Most of the people who hire me, I do natural light," he says. "You want to be there the half-hour, hour after sunrise, or the hour or half-hour before sunset."

PROPER PERSPECTIVE

When he photographs children or small dogs, he says he gets "high up to photograph them—how the world sees them. Generally the trick is getting at their level. I like to photograph a dog at eye level. But sometimes, shooting a Chihuahua or dachshund, I get on a ladder and shoot them from above."

Prepare an Evacuation Kit

You figure you've got the whole evacuation kit thing under control. The Band-Aids, flashlight, batteries, phone charger, drug prescriptions. Everyone knows where it's stored. You're prepared for anything, right?

Maybe. What about your insurance papers? Financial info?

"There are a number of things people forget, and one of the biggest things we see is the financial records," from insurance paperwork to banking information, says Jim Judge. "Those are things that are irreplaceable or take quite a bit of time to get replaced."

Judge is a paramedic, certified emergency manager based in Mount Dora, Fla., and on the American Red Cross' Scientific Advisory Council.

"Now is the time to get ready when it's sunny out and there's no danger on the horizon," Judge says. "You never know what's around the corner. You never know what's going to fall out of the sky. You never know what weather changes are going to bring."

Here are tips from Judge.

DEGREE OF DIFFICULTY: Easy. Unless you forgot where your insurance policy and bank records are stored—then the arrow moves to medium.

WHAT YOU NEED: Checklist, portable watertight storage container, computer to burn CDs or load USB flash drives.

EVACUATION KIT BASICS

The Red Cross lists some 40 items, including 1 gallon of water per person per day, food (protein and/or breakfast bars, easy-open cans), battery-powered or hand-crank radio, first-aid kit, multipurpose tool, emergency blanket, plus a contact card and personal documents (both are described below).

CUSTOMIZE

Add baby supplies, activities for children, extra pairs of eyeglasses, medic-alert tags. "And put (a kit) in the car," he adds. "You might not be home when something bad happens, so having a first-aid kit is important, but also items specific for your family."

PERSONAL INFORMATION

Include medication list, proof of address, copies of birth certificates, pet vaccination records, etc. Also insurance policies and banking information.

"You could always keep your backup information in a safety deposit box," Judge says, but remember, banks are often closed on weekends.

"A lot of this information can be backed up on a secure drive like a thumb drive or put on a CD. A lot of this information you can literally have in your back pocket. Make sure you use password protection encryption or whatever you can possibly use to protect that information."

CONTAINER

Consider a waterproof plastic bin or an old suitcase on wheels that has a handle. "You can put a lot of your information in that," Judge says, "and if something were to happen, you grab the suitcase, it's on wheels, it's easy to roll out."

CONTACT CARD

Every family member should carry one. The Red Cross website has a printable PDF: "People to Call or Text in an Emergency." It includes space for a meeting place outside the neighborhood as well as an out-of-area contact person. Why? Local phone lines may be overloaded or out of service.

COVERING ALL THE BASES

"Do more than cross your fingers" is a motto on the American Red Cross website (redcross.org), which has lots of information, from an online tutorial to an app. "Every one of those is vetted in science," says Red Cross board member Jim Judge. Among items you'll find: checklists (available as PDFs) for 24 situations, including earthquakes, floods, hurricanes, power outages, tornadoes, wildfires and winter storms. Go to redcross.org/preparednessfastfacts.

Summer First Aid for Kids

Worried about how to treat the little ones' warm-weather injuries? Here's what you should do—and what you shouldn't.

YOU CAN DO IT

BEE STING

Ice to the sting, ASAP. Then, try to get the stinger out once it's a tad numbed. Let the little guy know that within half an hour the pain will subside (obviously this works only for kids with a concept of time). Allergic reactions: Throat swelling, or body rash. If you see either of those, grab the Benadryl and call the doctor, or, if it's severe enough, dial 9-1-1.

TWISTED ANKLE

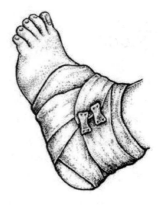

If a kid can't bear weight on it, it likely needs medical attention. Even if it's a minor sprain, get the kid off it. Try R-I-C-E, which spells rest, ice, compression, elevate. Use an ace bandage to secure an ice pack in place. If you do feel the need to slip on a pre-made compression wrap, make sure it's not too tight. You should be able to slip two fingers under the wrap. If the kid says he feels pins and needles below the wrap, it's too tight. And if the extremity turns bright red, it's too tight, and the blood can't return back to the heart.

SUNBURN

Remember, this is a first-degree burn. It's uncomfortable, and it's going to require local relief—a cool washcloth is best. Kids might benefit from some analgesic. Be prepared for a major peel.

SPLINTER

If you can't get it out with tweezers, in one solid piece or neat parts, don't be shy about getting medical help. "Don't ignore a splinter. It needs to come out."

GET TO THE DOCTOR ASAP IF THE KID...

- Has a head injury (Including a hard bonk on the head from a fall)

- Has an obviously deformed or immediately swollen body part

- Hits his/her abdomen hard against bike handlebars (You might not see the obvious fallout here, but there could be internal damage.)

- Needs stitches (Any time you can see the flesh beneath the skin, or if bleeding won't stop.)

- Steps on or is otherwise punctured by a rusty nail

Teach Bike Riding

Forget everything you think you know. Howard Roth, author of the e-book "Riding Made Easy" (ridingmadeeasy.com), takes that running-alongside-the-bike and balancing-on-training-wheels stuff and tosses it out the window. Says Roth, "The only people training wheels benefit are the people who make training wheels."

STEP 1: FIND A WIDE, OPEN SPACE

"Find a big empty parking lot with no parked cars, no curbs, no big lampposts. One with some very slight inclines is optimal," says Roth.

STEP 2: STRIKE A BALANCE

Buy a pedal wrench from a bike shop or hardware store and remove the pedals. Have the child sit on the bike, look forward (not down) and pick both feet off the ground an inch. "Let the bike fall to whatever side it's going to fall. It's only going to fall an inch." Do this until the child's feet are about six inches off the ground for three to five seconds at a time. "Bring your bike, too, and make it into a contest—who can (do it) the longest?"

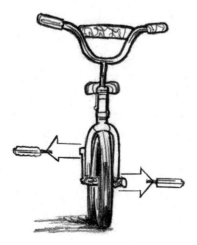

STEP 3: WALK THE BIKE

"Have them walk the bike, walk the bike, walk the bike until they start complaining they're getting bored. OK, let's go a little bit faster, a little bit faster, to the point where their feet can't keep up anymore and they're going to glide. At this point they get the feel of balancing, being on a moving bike and being in control because their feet are always near the ground and they can stop any time they want." Have them glide across the entire lot and back. "Keep doing this until they're bored. Bored means, 'Enough already, I'm ready for the next thing.'"

STEP 4: PUT THE PEDALS ON

Put the pedals back on the bike and position the pedals so they're parallel to the ground. "Tell them to put their feet on the pedals and pedal a little bit—just a rotation or two. This is where the kid says, 'Yeah, the hell with that, I'm not stopping.' And suddenly there they are, pedaling the bike while balancing."

MATERIALS: Cheap, small bike with foot brakes, knee, elbow guards, helmet, long-sleeve shirt, pants, pedal wrench

A kid is ready for this if he/she is able to...

- Stand on one foot for 5-10 seconds.
- Catch a large, soft ball from 5 feet away.
- Dodge a smaller ball tossed at him/her softly.

TECHNICAL

Change a Tire

When you get a flat tire, you don't need to be the helpless person on the side of the road waiting to be rescued. John Nielsen, director of auto repair services at AAA, describes how to safely change a car tire.

DEGREE OF DIFFICULTY: Medium

WHAT YOU NEED: Owners manual; spare tire (be sure you have a healthy one in the trunk); lug wrench; jack; towel and cotton gloves (optional; it's a dirty job).

STEP 1
Make sure you're well off the roadway and on a level, firm surface such as asphalt or concrete. Do not try to change a tire on a hill or soft surface like dirt or grass, because the jack could slip. Put on your hazard lights, and apply the emergency parking brake.

STEP 2
Using the lug wrench, loosen the lug nuts on the flat tire, but don't remove them completely. If you have a hubcap on the wheel, you'll have to remove that first, using the screwdriver-type tool on the opposite end of the lug wrench.

STEP 3
Install the jack under the car according to recommendations in the owners manual, which is usually in the glove compartment. Putting a jack in the wrong place could be ineffective or cause damage. Usually it goes under the frame near the flat tire.

STEP 4
Crank the jack's handle until the flat tire is 2 inches off the ground.

STEP 5

Finish taking off the lug nuts, and set them somewhere you won't lose them.

STEP 6

Putting your hands on the outside of the tire, lift slightly and pull it toward you. Tires can weigh 20 to 30 pounds, more on bigger trucks, so be careful. Roll the flat tire to the trunk. Remove the spare tire, and set the flat tire in its place.

STEP 7

Mount the spare tire onto the wheel hub, lining up the holes. Put the lug nuts back on, tightening only with your hands.

STEP 8

Lower jack until the new tire is on the ground. Remove jack; return it to the trunk.

STEP 9

Using the lug wrench, tighten one of the lug nuts until it's snug, then tighten the opposite nut on the other side of the tire. Tighten the remaining lug nuts. Do not tighten excessively; it could warp the brake rotors.

STEP 10

As quickly as possible, get your car to a tire shop to have the flat tire repaired or replaced.

Critical Car Checks

Hello, Ms. Acrylic Nails and Mr. But I'm Wearing a Nice Shirt. Did you guys know that aside from listening for thumping sounds or eyeing mysterious puddles of goo on the garage floor, there are things even the most automotively challenged car owners can do to maintain their vehicles? A little effort can keep your car safe and save money down the line.

DEGREE OF DIFFICULTY: The hardest part will be cleaning your hands after

WHAT YOU NEED: Wipers, Tire gauge, Necessary fluids, A rag

COST: $4 to $50

FLUID LEVELS

FREQUENCY
Check once a month, more frequently on older cars. Pop the hood and prop it up securely.

OIL AND TRANSMISSION
Check your owner's manual to find their locations. Remove the cap or dipstick, wipe it clean with a rag or paper towel, reinsert it, then withdraw it again. The "full" level is marked on the stick. Replenish fluids as necessary into the proper port, shown in the manual. And if the oil or fluid is dark, it probably needs to be changed. (Let a pro do it.)

WIPER FLUID & COOLANT
These are generally in opaque plastic reservoirs with obvious markings. The tops snap off for easy refilling.

ENGINE ON/OFF
Most fluid levels should be checked with the engine off and cold; it should be running when you check the transmission fluid. Beware of fan/belts.

WINDSHIELD WIPERS

FREQUENCY
Check twice a year, more frequently if you use a lot of washer fluid. Ask the pro at the auto parts store which wiper model fits your car.

REPLACE
Raise the wiper-arm assembly away from the windshield, then find the mounting clip. Release the clip (a screwdriver may be needed), and the wiper will slide off the arm. Slide the new wiper on until the mounting clip clicks, then lower the arm back to the windshield. Replace both wipers at the same time. (Change wipers, not just blades.)

TIRE PRESSURE

FREQUENCY
Check once a month. Get a tire gauge at any store with an auto section.

READING
Remove the cap on the tire's air valve—put it in your pocket so it doesn't get lost—then press the gauge to the valve. If you hear hissing, you're off; realign the gauge till it stops.

What's good? Newer cars will list tire pressure on a sticker usually inside the driver's door or doorjamb. That figure may not jibe with the tire manufacturer's specifications though. Go with the manufacturer's (check the tire, go online or ask a tire dealer). Get air at the gas station.

NOTE
Slightly underinflated tires may make for a smoother ride, but they cut your mileage and shorten the life of your tires.

Display the American Flag

If you plan to let your patriotic colors fly on Memorial Day, do right by Old Glory and display it with dignity—which is to say, not on your stars-and-stripes bikini. The U.S. Flag Code gives guidelines for properly displaying the American flag. The rules are purely advisory and there's no enforcement or penalty for violating them, though there are some exceptions for the District of Columbia and states can make their own flag laws.

DEGREE OF DIFFICULTY: Easy

1. Whether hanging horizontally or vertically, the union should be uppermost and to the observer's left (in a window, the observer is the person in the street).

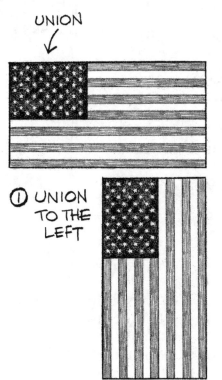

2. On Memorial Day, the flag should fly at half-staff until noon and then be hoisted to the peak. (When flying at half-staff, hoist the flag to the peak first before lowering it to half-staff; bring to the peak again before bringing it down for the day).

MEMORIAL DAY PROCEDURE

① RAISE FLAG TO TOP AND THEN DOWN TO HALF UNTIL NOON.

② BRING FLAG TO PEAK.

③ LOWER AT SUNSET

U.S. FLAG IS ALWAYS ABOVE OTHER FLAGS

3. The flag should be displayed outside from sunrise to sunset only, unless it's properly illuminated at night.

4. When displayed with other national flags, all flags should be the same size and fly from separate staffs of the same height.

5. When displayed with other state, local or society flags, the U.S. flag should always be at the peak (if on the same halyard—the rope that hoists the flag); at the center and highest point (if in a cluster of staffs); and hoisted first and lowered last (if on adjacent flag poles). No other flag should be above it or to the flag's own right.

6. From crossed staffs, the U.S. flag should be on the observer's left, with its staff in front.

7. When marching, the flag should be carried on the marching right, or, if there's a line of flags, in front of the center of that line.

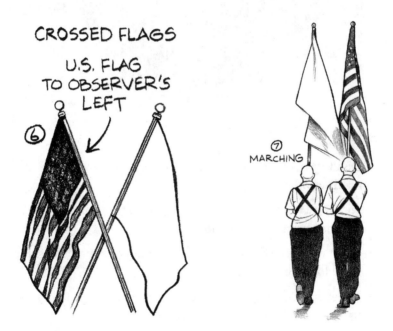

CROSSED FLAGS

U.S. FLAG
TO OBSERVER'S
LEFT

⑥

⑦
MARCHING

8. On a car, the flag staff should be fixed to the chassis or clamped to the right fender.

9. Wear a flag lapel pin over your heart.

FOLDING THE FLAG: Though the Flag Code does not specify how the flag should be folded, tradition dictates you end up with a triangle with only the blue union showing. For instructions, visit legion.org/flag/folding.

PROPERLY
FOLDED FLAG

FLAG NO-NOS

- Don't display the flag during inclement weather (unless it's an all-weather flag).
- Never let the flag touch anything beneath it, including the ground, water or merchandise.
- Don't drape the flag over vehicles, wear it as apparel or use it as bedding or drapery.
- Never carry the flag flat or horizontal, or festoon it or draw it up in folds. It should fly aloft and free.
- Never put any mark, insignia, words, pictures or designs on the flag.

Fix a Leaky Faucet

One drip per second from a leaky faucet equals 3,000 to 8,000 gallons of wasted water a year, according to Paul Patton, senior product manager for Delta Faucet, and Chuck White, vice president of technical and code services for the Plumbing-Heating-Cooling Contractors Association.

Plus, water is big-time corrosive, "more like sand than oil," says White. That leak is corroding the metal parts deep inside your faucet, and that's the aim of your fix-it. May be nothing more than a loose ring that needs tightening, or you may need to ditch the innards, a part called "the seat," or in a newfangled faucet, "the cartridge." That's the part that needs to be swapped out. Either that, or start fresh with a whole new faucet. In which case, you may want to call a plumber.

Here are tips from White and Patton.

DEGREE OF DIFFICULTY: Tricky enough to show why plumbers were invented.

WHAT YOU NEED: Screwdriver, needle-nose pliers, adjustable wrench, Allen wrench. And depending on your replacement part, the correct "seat removing tool" (with a hexagon fitting, or a square protruding from the end). Without the right removing tool, you're, well, soaked.

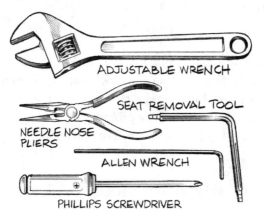

ADJUSTABLE WRENCH

SEAT REMOVAL TOOL

NEEDLE NOSE PLIERS

ALLEN WRENCH

PHILLIPS SCREWDRIVER

STEP 1

Turn off the water. Also, plug the sink so you don't lose parts down the drain.

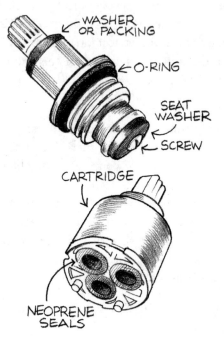

STEP 2

Identify the brand and model of the faucet so you buy the right parts. Thirty years ago, most of the market was washer-and-seat, says Patton. Now, many manufacturers have eliminated those two parts for what's known as a cartridge.

STEP 3

Faucets come in single- or two-handle varieties; for two-handle you must determine whether the leak is coming from the hot or cold side (put your finger under the drip; you'll know). Stick to the side that's the source of the problem, or, as long as you're at it, replace the innards on both the hot and cold.

STEP 4

Remove the faucet handle with a screwdriver or Allen wrench.

STEP 5

On a single-handle faucet, you'll now see a metal ring; tighten it with needle-nose pliers. If you're lucky, this will fix the leak; if not, forge on. But because single-handle faucets vary by brand, your best bet is to follow specific instructions that come with the replacement parts.

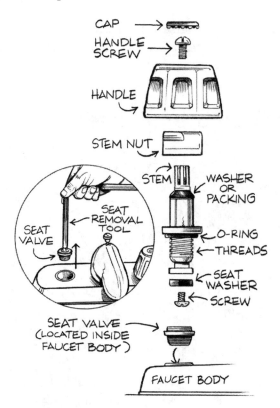

CAP

HANDLE SCREW

HANDLE

STEM NUT

STEM

WASHER OR PACKING

SEAT REMOVAL TOOL

SEAT VALVE

O-RING

THREADS

SEAT WASHER

SCREW

SEAT VALVE (LOCATED INSIDE FAUCET BODY)

FAUCET BODY

STEP 6

For a two-handle faucet, you'll see a nut. Remove it. See that sticking-up stem? Pull the stem straight out, and with it comes the cartridge. If it's an older seat-and-washer gizmo, just turn the stem open to lift out the stem and washer. Look down into the hole (you may need a flashlight) to see the seat. If it's shiny and smooth, it's OK; if it's not, it's the source of your troubles. Unscrew it with the seat-removing tool.

STEP 7

Once the old parts are yanked, replace with either a new cartridge or new, identical seat. And use the proper tool (likely a six-sided Allen wrench or a four-sided wrench); don't forget to replace the washer too.

STEP 8

Reinstall the parts in reverse order. Turn on the water; now turn it off. Don't hear that telltale drip? You're a plumbing star.

Jump Start a Car Battery

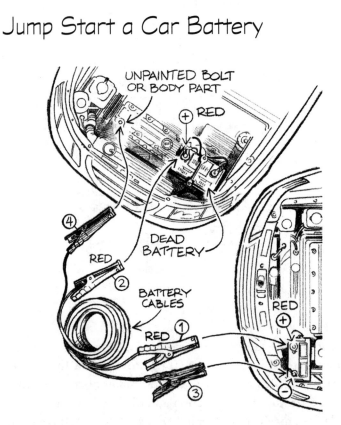

It always seems to happen when you're late. You turn your car's ignition and hear the dreaded silence of a dead battery.

The best option is to carry a self-contained battery jumper, said Lauren Fix, spokeswoman for the Car Care Council (carcare. org), a consumer education campaign. A portable jump starter can be juiced up in a wall socket and left in your trunk; it clamps onto the dead battery and delivers the charge needed to start a car. Many models cost less than $100.

Barring such foresight, find another car to give you a jump, which takes some knowledge of cable connections and battery health so you don't shock yourself or, in rare cases, cause an explosion.

Fix, an ASE (Automotive Service Excellence)-certified technician, describes how.

Important note: These instructions may not apply to all hybrid vehicles. If you have an electric or hybrid car, follow directions in the owners manual.

DEGREE OF DIFFICULTY: Medium.

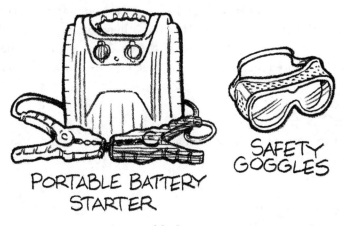

PORTABLE BATTERY
STARTER

SAFETY
GOGGLES

WHAT YOU NEED: A portable battery starter streamlines the process. Otherwise, battery cables, a volunteer car with a working battery, goggles.

STEP 1

Pull the assisting car up to the dead car close enough so the cables can reach but not so close that the cars touch. Turn off headlights, blinkers, radios and heating systems, and unplug accessories from power sockets on the dead car.

STEP 2

Pop the hoods. Locate the batteries in each car and identify the positive (+) and negative (-) terminals. Wear goggles to protect your eyes in case of explosion.

STEP 3

Identify the jumper cables: Red is for the positive charge, black for the negative. The thicker the cables, the better the jump. Don't let the clamps of the opposing cables touch, or you may get a shock.

STEP 4

Take the red jumper cable and affix one clamp to the positive post of the dead car battery. Affix the other clamp of the red cable to the positive post of the live car battery.

STEP 5

Take the black jumper cable and affix one clamp to the negative post of the live car battery. Affix the other clamp of the black cable NOT to the negative post of the dead battery, but rather to an unpainted metal part of the dead car's engine block, such as a bolt. Otherwise you might get a jolt.

STEP 6

Start the engine of the assisting car. Start the dead car. Once it cranks, leave it running for a few minutes to draw the charge from the good battery.

STEP 7

With both cars running, remove the cables in the reverse order from which you placed them. (And take your car to get your battery checked.)

SAFETY FIRST

Do not attempt to jump a car if:

You smell gas or acid; see the battery leaking liquid or see an electrical spark; or the battery has come out of the battery tray. Instead, call a tow truck to take it to a technician.

Load a Truck on Moving Day

STEP LADDER FOR HANDLING
ITEMS ABOVE CHEST LEVEL

BACK

FRONT WALL

POSITION HEAVY
APPLIANCES / ITEMS
AGAINST FRONT
WALL

LIGHT ITEMS↑

HEAVY ITEMS↓

Books

RAMP   DESIGNATE
A 'SUPERVISOR'   MOVING
PADS   PUSH ITEMS
TIGHT
TOGETHER

Packing a moving truck is like cutting your own hair. The more you do it, the better you'll be at it. (One common pointer: The chance for success increases substantially if you keep the beer on ice until the work is done.) Here are tips to help things go more smoothly:

In a perfect world, all the boxes would be the same size. "But the reality is they're not," says Dean Schroeder, a 33-year veteran of United Parcel Service, where he trains the managers who train the people who load the trailers. "Ideally, if you have a choice, it would be good to have them all the same size and shape."

Load the heaviest items first: a fridge or piano. Move them to the front of the truck, and equalize the weight. Use moving pads or blankets to cover furniture and prevent damage (pillows, comforters, towels and cushions make good padding too). Break down what you can (bed frames, for example) and fit them in where there's space.

You want a snug fit, so things are held in place. But not so compacted that boxes get crushed and items damaged.

If you're moving just boxes, start loading from the front of the truck to the back. Begin with what Schroeder calls a cornerstone. "It's the package that sets the depth and height of your wall, and it's a sturdy one," he says. "Maybe 18 to 24 inches wide, by 12 to 24 high. That package is usually touching the last wall, the end of the trailer, and that sets the depth."

UPS trains its crews to work from left to right. Put the cornerstone on the left side, then the next package should be the same height.

Heavier and sturdier packages go on the bottom, lighter ones on top. Build at least three shelves of boxes, rather than one tall (and unstable) column. For anything stacked above chest level, use a small stepladder.

Designate a loader. Others assisting with the move can bring things out to the truck, but it works best if one person is inside fitting pieces together and acting as the team quarterback.

Use all the space, not only so things don't shift during transit, but also for efficiency purposes. "Smaller packages are used as filler," Schroeder says. "If I have packages of different sizes, I may have space between or behind. I'm filling that space with smaller packages while I'm still building the shelves."

Make a Campfire Without Matches

When unforeseen circumstances leave you stranded, it's handy to know how to start a campfire without matches or a lighter. "It

WHAT'S NEEDED

1 10' AREA CLEARED OF FLAMMABLE MATERIAL

ROCKS

2

B KINDLING

C LARGER STICKS/LOGS

A TINDER BUNDLE

is not easy," warns Denise Long, a wilderness survival instructor and author of "Survivor Kid" (Chicago Review Press, $12.95). But if cavemen could do it, you can too. Here's her advice.

DEGREE OF DIFFICULTY: Hard

Prepare an area: Clear about 10 feet, not on grass and away from overhanging branches. Make a ring with rocks, to contain the flames. Don't choose rocks that have been alongside a river; they may have water-filled cracks that can explode when heated. Gather materials to help light and feed the fire. You'll need a tinder bundle that you light first—anything dry and flammable, such as dried grass, pine needles, strips of bark, paper, dried animal droppings. Gather enough to make a fluffy bundle the size of a bird's nest. You also will need kindling—tiny twigs and small pieces of dry wood to feed the initial flames—and slightly larger sticks and logs to feed the fire once it starts.

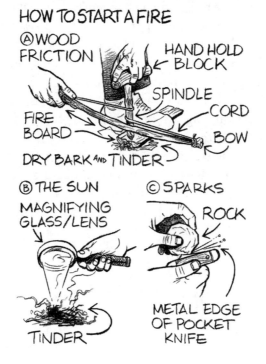

HOW TO START A FIRE

Ⓐ WOOD FRICTION — HAND HOLD BLOCK — SPINDLE — CORD — FIRE BOARD — BOW — DRY BARK AND TINDER

Ⓑ THE SUN — MAGNIFYING GLASS/LENS — TINDER

Ⓒ SPARKS — ROCK — METAL EDGE OF POCKET KNIFE

Create Fire Without Matches

Wood friction: By rubbing two pieces of dry wood together, you generate smoke and, eventually, an ember that you slide into your tinder bundle. Blow gently to create a flame. The most effective method is to use a bow drill, a contraption you construct of wood and cord to give you greater speed and friction and protect your hands from blisters. Visit bit.ly/k5etrS for detailed instructions.

You can start a fire with anything highly reflective, such as a magnifying glass, eyeglasses, camera lens, a mirror, the back of a CD. Angle the glass or mirror so sunlight reflects onto the tinder bundle. Eventually it will smoke and turn into flame. The catch: It has to be sunny for this to work.

Striking certain rocks together, such as flint, against steel (like the back of a pocket knife) can produce sparks. Angle the sparks toward the tinder, then blow gently to help it catch. Long recommends carrying a magnesium block on a key chain; magnesium shavings catch fire easily with a spark, even when wet. The block has a flint strip on one side so you don't need to worry about finding a piece of flint.

KEEP IT GOING: Once the tinder is aflame, gently feed the fire with the kindling. As the fire gets going, add the larger sticks, and finally the logs.

Put it out! Forest fires can start from improperly extinguished campfires. Be sure your fire is out before you leave. The best method: Pour water on top of it and stir with a stick to snuff out all embers hidden below. You can also cover it with a thick layer of dirt or sand.

Smarter Lawn Mowing

Thomas Christopher is a lawn and garden expert calling for a radical revamp of how we approach yard care. "Lawns. I keep struggling with them," says Christopher, editor of the just-published "The New American Landscape: Leading Voices on the Future of Sustainable Gardening" (Timber Press, $34.95). "I try to persuade people to do it in an easier, more environmental way, but people are stuck back in the Eisenhower years.

"It's got to stop," he added. "People have to get a grip and break the habit."

Here are some ways to break turf's hold on your life, resulting in a greener and "greener" lawn that takes far less time to maintain.

DEGREE OF DIFFICULTY: Executing these tips is easier than letting go of old habits.

Make sure the mower blade is very sharp. "A dull blade leaves grass looking ragged and encourages disease or lawn problems," Christopher says.

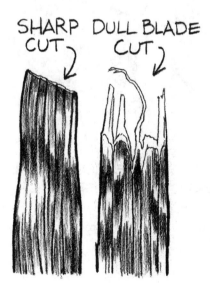

SHARP CUT   DULL BLADE CUT

SET THE MOWER LEVEL HIGHER.

"Most people set their lawn mowers way too short," he says, noting too close a cut damages the grass, encourages weed growth and calls for too-frequent mowing. It's never about how short the grass is but how neat and trim the lawn looks when finished. Grass varieties grown in cooler climes should be 3 inches long or longer; warm-climate grasses, such as Bermuda and centipede grasses, can be cut a bit shorter, to around 1½ inches.

LET YOUR MOWER "DESIGN" THE YARD

Once you start the mower rolling, do not back up or make, in Christopher's words, "turns so tight they require slowing down." When you finish, look around for any areas of uncut grass. "The trick is to eliminate the little corners, peninsulas and island of grass," says Christopher. "Those patches are time-waster areas." What to do then? Don't mow those patches; replace with ground covers or mulch.

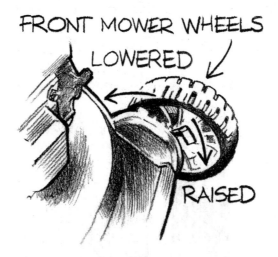

START MOWING IN THE MOST VISIBLE AREA OF THE PROPERTY, LIKE THE FRONT LAWN

Christopher says the most efficient way to mow is to choose a specific area and mow in a circular motion from the edges toward the center. Mowing back and forth in rows is also acceptable.

LET NO SINGLE BUSH OR TREE BE AN ISLAND IN YOUR YARD

If there's something planted in the middle of the lawn that makes mowing hard, like a large bush with overarching branches, Christopher recommends ripping out the grass under the bush. Create a garden bed or plant some more bushes. Use mulch to create a large, even shape that's easy to mow around. "Don't drop plants into your yard," he warns.

BE AWARE OF YOUR TERRAIN, ESPECIALLY ANY STEEP SLOPES.

Christopher had a friend who was mowing downhill, slipped, and his feet went under the mower. "He lost a couple of toes," Christopher recalls. Where the ground goes downhill, mow back and forth across the grade.

CREATE LARGE MULCHED AREAS

FOLLOW CONTOURS OF AREA TO BE MOWED

DON'T BE OVEREAGER ABOUT MOWING.

Christopher has encountered a number of guys who can't cut back on their grass-cutting routine even when their yards really don't need it. Be honest about whether or not you can give up the mower.

Take/Throw a Punch

It's not a skill you trot out to show the neighbors, or something you demonstrate at family gatherings or PTA meetings. But when you need to know about punching and being punched, you call Earnie Shavers. The former heavyweight boxer is generally considered the hardest puncher of his generation, better than Muhammad Ali and Joe Frazier. Of Shavers' 74 career victories, 68 were by knockout. Now 65, he lives in Houston, is employed by a sporting goods company and has a prison ministry.

THROWING THE PUNCH

THE FIST

Make a fist like you're holding a pitcher. "Lay the thumb outside, across the knuckles," Shavers says. "If you put it inside, it's very easy to get broken."

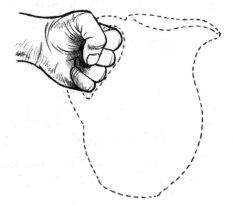

THE STANCE

"Not real wide," he says. "I'd say probably a foot, maybe shoulder width."

The shorter and quicker the better. "All you need is a 6-inch punch," Shavers says. The longer your punch, the more time your opponent has to block it. Also follow through; don't throw a 6-inch punch and stop. Punch through the target. "You don't try to reach his jaw; you punch through it."

THE MOVEMENT

When Shavers was starting out, his trainer taught him to get all the power out of his punches by pivoting, "I stepped in with a left, put my left foot out. Step in, you turn. Your power comes from the back and leg muscles. To get that power you have to twist your body. Snapping it, snapping it." When landing the punch, turn your wrist clockwise a half turn.

THE TARGET

The head is the best target, Shavers says, above the eyes to stun your opponent. Or the jaw. Follow the short jab with a second punch right behind it. "Bam-bam!" he explains. "I was always taught, most times, a guy is going to duck down. Aim for his throat and he'll duck right into it."

TAKE A PUNCH

"If you have to take a punch, you should have your jaw tightened (like on a mouthpiece). If you have your mouth open you'll probably have your jaw broken."

Try to deflect it. Try to throw a jab.

Twist or turn to make it a glancing blow.

"You won't take all the power then, won't take the full force."

You want to brace yourself. Yes.

Unclog a Bathroom Drain

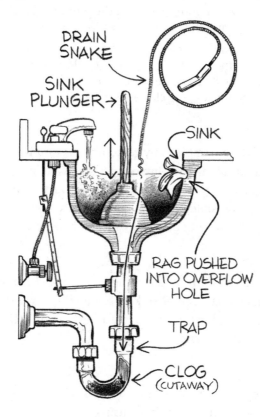

DRAIN
SNAKE

SINK
PLUNGER→

SINK

RAG PUSHED
INTO OVERFLOW
HOLE

TRAP

CLOG
(CUTAWAY)

The lavatory sink is the likeliest clog in the house, says lifelong plumber Chuck White, vice president of technical and code services for the Plumbing-Heating-Cooling Contractors Association, a national trade group based in Falls Church, Va. And you can probably unclog it without bringing in a plumber, White says. (Unlike kitchen sinks, which are usually clogged by food bits—as opposed to a tangle of hairs—and often tied into a disposal, making them a tough job for do-it-yourselfers.)

DEGREE OF DIFFICULTY: Medium—if it's the bathroom we're talking about. If, however, every drain in the house is backing up, this is over your head. Call the plumber. Kitchen sink clogged to a standstill? Most likely a job for a plumber.

WHAT YOU NEED: Sink plunger (just like the toilet plunger, only shrunken to fit over the sink drain), Old rag, Drain snake (available at most hardware stores, but this moves you up into the advanced unclogging class), Plumber's phone number

STEP 1

First, refrain from dumping any goo down the drain. And if you do and wind up calling the plumber, be honest about what you poured. Someone could get hurt; these products can contain noxious stuff that could burn skin and produce toxic fumes, especially if combined with other off-the-shelf potions.

STEP 2

Before you start pushing on the plunger, plug the overflow drain (that peephole in the actual sink, often just under the faucet) with the rag—but don't let it slide into the hole. This closes the circuit and creates suction.

STEP 3

Time for the sink plunger—it's about half the size of the toilet variety. Do not even think about using the toilet plunger. It's gross, and it's too big to form a tight seal around the sink drain.

STEP 4

But if that doesn't work, try the drain snake, which is basically a hand crank and cable. You snake it down the drain opening, then turn the crank. It takes some finesse. Apartment dwellers: If your sink and your neighbor's drain into the same pipe, you might snake through to the sink on the other side of the wall. Careful.

STEP 5

Still not unclogged? Call the plumber.

SOCIAL

Apologize

Apologizing isn't so much an art as a sport. When approached as a skill to build, governed by a few simple rules, the apology almost always achieves its goal—despite any fumbles during delivery. When it's over, everyone wins.

DEGREE OF DIFFICULTY: Medium to hard, depending on aversion to eye contact.

STEP 1

FORGET DODGE BALL; APOLOGIZING IS A CONTACT SPORT

"Eye-to-eye, face-to-face, that's the one way it works," said Maribeth Kuzmeski, author of "The Engaging Child" (Red Zone Publishing) and "The Connectors" (Wiley), both relationship skills books. "My son, when he was younger,...(would) write a note of apology. We would say, 'We're so happy you took the time to write us this note. We'd really like you to talk to us about it.'"

Now, her kids and their peers apologize by text message. "That seems to be accepted. Apologies are situational sometimes. But, as a parent, if my daughter apologized by text message to me, I would say, 'Are you kidding me?' Teenager to teenager may be one way, but teen to adult or adult to adult, if you really mean it, you go face-to-face and suck it up."

STEP 2

FIND A SEGUE.

Rolling into the apology is often the toughest part, especially if the tone up to now has been light. Kuzmeski suggests a transitional, "Hey, I wanted to talk to you about something." That signals the subject matter is important. Next you might say, "I know you were unhappy with something that I did, and I'd like to talk to you about that."

STEP 3

INCLUDE THE "I," AS IN "I'M SORRY," NOT JUST "SORRY."
The latter is the equivalent of "Love ya!" versus "I love you." It's often employed by kids who feel justified in what they did. "We need to teach, if something they've done has upset the other person, and they don't want the person upset, then they say an authentic apology," Kuzmeski said. "Hopefully we can get to the point where they're sorry for what (the misunderstanding) has done, if not sorry for what they've done."

STEP 4

DON'T QUALIFY IT.
 Banish the "if" and "but," as in, "I'm sorry if I hurt your feelings but your outfit reminded me of dad's Naugahyde recliner." Those qualifiers/justifiers will bury a deeper hole. If you can't apologize without them, don't apologize.

"We have to apologize in a believable way and not have any other messages intertwined in there," Kuzmeski said.

If you're unclear of your offense, however, it's OK to say, "I see I hurt your feelings. I don't completely understand. Can you tell me what you're feeling?" If there was a misunderstanding or oversensitivity in your view, mend the fence with, "I didn't know it would make you feel the way it did or I never would have said it. That wasn't my intention. I'm sorry."

STEP 5

DON'T EXPECT INSTANT ABSOLUTION.
"You want the other person to tell you it's OK. And they may not do that," she said. Perhaps your apology lacked conviction; you may wish to reiterate how sorry you are and add, if it's a personal relationship (not business), "Will you please forgive me?" If the person replies, "Stop apologizing—it's over already!" do stop. The person may just need time.

THE APOLOGY UNDER DURESS: Kuzmeski condones requiring a child to apologize, a la, "If you want to do whatever the next thing is that you want to do, you have to apologize to your sister." "If you wait till they really feel sorry, you might be waiting 10 years," she said. "What's more important is to get them to know that apologizing is the right thing to do. It's social intelligence type of teaching."

HOW TO RECEIVE AN APOLOGY

You don't have to say, "Oh, that's OK." Especially if you're still sore. Kids are known to fire back at an apologizer with "Well, I don't forgive you!" A more mature alternative: "Thank you for apologizing."

Ask for a Favor

Asking for a favor isn't always easy, but it is rewarding. Not only do you get the assurance that someone will pick up your mail or check in on your cat, but you also get the great feeling that you're part of a larger community of people who are looking out for each other and pitching in to make each others' lives easier.

So how do you get started?

"The best way to get what you want is to help other people get what they want," says Mary Mitchell, author of "The Complete Idiot's Guide to Etiquette" (Alpha).

"Role-model being willing to help," she adds. "Then you have the right to ask other people to help you."

You might, for instance, pick up on your neighbor's concern about last-minute trip preparations and offer to put his garbage cans out on the street. If your friend mentions a scheduling conflict, you can offer to pick up her kids from school along with your own.

"This is all about nurturing relationships, and if your antennae are up about the other guy, what might really help that person, it's nice to offer (a favor)," says Mitchell, who offers these tips.

DETERMINE IF YOUR REQUEST IS REASONABLE.

The question to ask yourself: "If the shoes were on the other feet, would I want to do this?" If you would happily watch your friend's kids for an hour, you're on firm ground. If her kids hate your kids and you would rather clip a newborn's toenails than deal with the angst that's likely to result from a group get-together, you should probably refrain from asking your friend to host one.

ASK IN A TIMELY MANNER.

Have you seen those office posters that say "Lack of planning on your part does not constitute an emergency on my part?" That slogan is worth keeping in mind. "Don't put the other person in such a time crunch that it becomes a huge imposition," Mitchell says.

ASK BY PHONE OR FACE-TO-FACE.

This is one of those times when it's important to make a personal connection; texting generally isn't appropriate.

GIVE THE OTHER PERSON A WAY OUT.

Mitchell might say, "I'd be so grateful if you could (do this favor for me). Is that something that might work on your end?" Note how she phrases that last sentence. It's hard for someone to say they can't do something for you. It's easier for them to say something "wouldn't work" for them at a particular time.

DON'T GO NEGATIVE.

Avoid wording such as, "I totally understand if you can't do this," which anticipates rejection and downplays the other person's willingness to help. Mitchell sees a parallel with the person who argues with a compliment ("Oh, this old thing? I hate the way I look in it.") The compliment-denier is effectively belittling the judgment of the poor person who stuck their neck out and said, "That shirt looks great on you." It's much better to smile, say "Thank you," and move on when you get a compliment—and much better to stress how grateful you'd be when you ask for a favor.

RESPOND GRACIOUSLY.

If the other person says no, you can say, "I understand. Thanks for considering." If the other person says yes, "Oh! You're wonderful!" works well.

Be a Good Witness to a Crime

When a crime happens, most folks will act like Clark Kent, not Superman. That's OK; dialing for help and reporting what you're seeing can be heroic too.

"If you see a crime occurring, call 911. Don't intervene," says Jenny Shearer, a spokeswoman with the FBI's national press office in Washington, D.C. "You have to keep your personal safety in mind too. Don't take undue risk.

"Observe what you can. Could you identify that person again? If there's a car involved, can you make out the license plate, make or model? Any information you can provide helps."

Witnesses unwilling to "get involved" can always report crime activity anonymously, said Michelle L. Boykins, communications director for the National Crime Prevention Council (ncpc.org) in Arlington, Va. Many police departments have anonymous-tip telephone hotlines or cellphone texting options for witnesses, she said.

"In talking anecdotally to law enforcement, we know people are using these anonymous reporting mechanisms," Boykins said. "(They) are happy to get those tips so they can bring perpetrators in."

Do take care before you use your cell phone's camera during a crime. "The best eyewitness is a live witness so (the council) does not recommend you put yourself in harm's way to snap a cell phone picture of the criminal," Boykins said. "If you can safely snap a picture of a license plate, that is great, but you must do so without putting yourself at risk."

WHAT YOU NEED: Calm under fire and a cell phone or access to a phone.

DEGREE OF DIFFICULTY: Medium-low: Accurate recall is key, but you'll be remembering details under duress.

STEP 1
Call 911 if a crime has occurred or is in progress, if you recognize a wanted criminal and for all vehicle crashes.

STEP 2
Stay calm, speak clearly.

STEP 3
Give a brief description of the crime.

STEP 4
Provide time of the crime.

STEP 5
Share your exact location.

STEP 6
Tell the operator the extent of injuries or damage.

STEP 7
Provide description(s) of the suspect(s), including race, height, weight, clothing, hair color/style, facial hair, scars/marks/tattoos.

STEP 8
Give a description of any weapons used.

STEP 9
Provide a description of suspect's vehicle, including make, model, color and tag numbers.

STEP 10
Tell direction of flight (east, west, down an alley or street) and mode of transportation (car, bike or on foot).

STEP 11
Do not hang up until the call-taker tells you it is OK.

STEP 12
Know the telephone number you are calling from.

SOURCE: National Crime Prevention Council

STRENGTHEN YOUR MEMORY

How can you "train" yourself to be a better witness? Michelle L. Boykins, communications and marketing director of the National Crime Prevention Council, recommends a game of "What if?"

___

"Can you recall what your spouse or kids were wearing when they left the house this morning?" she asked. "If you are in a bank or a convenience store, can you describe the people in the store? Did you notice any tattoos or other distinguishing features?"

Break the Ice

Oh fun, a holiday party. Cue the awkward silence as you stand beside a fellow partygoer with whom your only shared interest appears to be the bean dip.

___

Margaret Shepherd, author of "The Art of Civilized Conversation" (Broadway), offered pointers for how to gracefully break the ice to start a good dialogue—an exercise far more enjoyable when you don't view it as networking to get ahead, she notes, but as a chance to learn something interesting.

"It's an opportunity to really connect with somebody," she said.

IF YOU DON'T KNOW ANYONE

Ask the host if there's anyone he/she thinks you should meet, and request an introduction. Don't whine that you don't know anyone and glue yourself to the host's side all night, because then you're just annoying.

IF YOU DON'T KNOW WHAT TO SAY

Rub two clichés together. Rather than revert to predictable observations, like the awfulness of the weather or the attractiveness of someone's coat, combine two banal topics into something more personal, such as: "That's a beautiful color you've got on, it warms me up just to look at it." Everyone loves to be praised.

NO, REALLY, YOU DON'T KNOW WHAT TO SAY

After sticking your hand out and introducing yourself, you must cover three basic points before moving on to any more meaningful conversation. 1. Ask a question ("How do you know the host?"). 2. State a fact about yourself ("I live next door"). 3. State an opinion ("This bean dip is amazing."). Only after laying that groundwork can you broach deeper topics.

IF YOU'RE ITCHING TO TALK ABOUT THE REPUBLICAN PRIMARY

Resist! Good manners dictate that with new acquaintances you should steer clear of discussing politics, religion, money or sex—which may seem like antiquated advice, but more often than not those topics set the conversation down a negative path.

"Almost everyone wants to convince you of their beliefs, and almost no one wants to hear yours," Shepherd said. "It's best to focus on topics that will let you grow and where the other person is likely to meet you halfway."

IF YOU FIND YOURSELF RAMBLING

Be sure to "boomerang" the conversation to allow the other person to talk, perhaps by asking if they've had a similar experience to yours. People are happier talking about themselves.

IF YOU'RE TALKING TO CHILDREN

Resist the urge to note how much they've grown or remember how obsessed they were with Webkins at your last meeting. Rather than push a kid back to his or her younger self, focus on the present: "I haven't seen you in two years; you must have grown into some new interests that I need to catch up on."

IF YOUR EFFORTS ARE FALLING FLAT

Don't take it personally, as some people are really shy. And don't be afraid of silence. Stand shoulder-to-shoulder, rather than face-to-face, which is less intimidating and allows you to people-watch together.

LAUNCHING CONVERSATIONS

The key to get a conversation rolling is to ask questions—and really listen to the answers so you can follow up (don't let your mind wander 10 seconds in). There are five general categories:
1. A person's journey. (What brought you to this city?)
2. The recent past. (How is business nowadays?)
3. Travel. (Any interesting trips planned?)
4. The current situation you're sharing at that moment. (What did you think of that speech?)
5. Companions. (Do you have family in the area?)

Choose an Engagement Ring

Like wondering whether she'll say yes isn't stressful enough. You're also supposed to select and purchase a ring that fits her magnificent personality, her singular style and her, ahem, finger? Help! We called on the Engagement Experts (engagement-experts.com) to do just that. If you're still flummoxed, ask her (trustworthy) friend to advise.

STEP 1: KNOW THE FOUR C'S

CUT

Proportions determine brilliance and sparkle. Grades are assigned based on these. (Don't confuse cut with shape.)

- SHALLOW: Looks bigger from top, light escapes out the bottom

- IDEAL: Light enters, exits through top; most expensive
- DEEP: Light exits the sides; usually a higher carat weight

CLARITY
Ranks internal imperfections, called inclusions (I). Only grades I 1-I 3 have inclusions visible to the naked eye.

COLOR
A letter-grade scale rating the absence of color.

CARAT WEIGHT
This is how much the diamond weighs. 1carat = 100 points. Bigger number = higher cost. (Bigger isn't always better.) Also consider the top of the diamond in millimeters, which determines how big it looks in the setting.

STEP 2: SHAPE, SETTING

SHAPE
Rounds are the most popular, but pick what she'll love.

SETTING
Anything your heart desires. Top metals are yellow gold (10K, 14K, 18K), white gold (needs replating over time), and platinum (hypoallergenic and most expensive).

STEP 3: KNOW YOUR GIRLFRIEND
Ask yourself: What do her favorite jewelry pieces look like? Are they more contemporary? Classic? Vintage looking? Are they big and bold pieces or more understated? How does she dress? Would you classify her as bold, earthy, vintage, classic or elegant?

STEP 4: KNOW HER RING SIZE
If she wears a ring on her ring finger, grab it next time it's off. Place it on a piece of paper, run a pencil around the inside and take the drawing to the jeweler, who can turn your reconnaissance into an actual size. Or, go costume jewelry shopping. Have her try on a variety of rings on different fingers, keeping in mind which one fits her ring finger. Buy it for later reference.

Door Etiquette

Who opens the door for whom? Even if your mom told you—and you actually paid attention—the old rules are evolving. Sue Fox, author of "Etiquette for Dummies," offers advice for the modern era.

THE STANDARD DOOR

MAN AND WOMAN

Traditionally, the man would open the door for the woman, and that's still fine to do, but no longer widely expected. Today, the one who arrives at the door first opens it and holds it open for the other person—regardless of gender.

MAN AND MAN

Again, the person who arrives first opens the door and holds it, unless one of the men happens to be elderly or his arms are full with packages.

WOMAN AND WOMAN

Same as man-man.

MAN WHO INSISTS ON OPENING THE DOOR FOR A WOMAN

The woman may think the courtesy is dated, but it's still a courtesy. She should say, "Thank you."

ELDERLY PERSON AND YOUNGER ADULT

The more capable person opens the door.

BOSS AND EMPLOYEE

Rank does apply here. Junior executives open doors for senior executives. If your boss happens to reach for the door ahead of you, be gracious, don't fight over who gets to open door and remember to say, "Thank you."

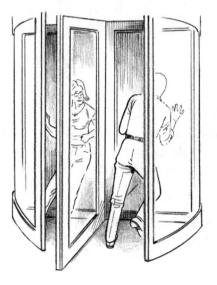

THE REVOLVING DOOR

MAN AND WOMAN

Traditionally, a man would let the woman enter a moving door first, enter the section behind her, and push to keep the door moving. If the revolving door wasn't moving, he would enter first and push. Today, whoever arrives first enters first and pushes. If a door is heavy, the man may want to go first and push for the woman. But it's fine for women to go first.

MAN AND MAN

Whoever arrives first goes first. If you arrive together, the man who is younger would let the elder man go first, unless the elder man needed assistance with the door.

WOMAN AND WOMAN

Whoever arrives first goes first. If one of the women is elderly and needs assistance, the younger woman goes first to push the door.

ADULT AND CHILD

The adult goes first.

BOSS AND EMPLOYEE

The higher ranking person enters first.

Drive in a Funeral

Consider this tip from an eHow.com Web entry on how to drive in a funeral procession: "Do not do anything illegal while driving, such as drinking beer. Do not think that the police officers guiding you will let you get away with such behavior."

Drinking beer in a funeral procession. Really?

Unfortunately, most of us would not be surprised. Funeral etiquette has almost expired in this anything-goes age. And riding in a cortege is far too often a frightening experience as the bereaved must contend with impatient, ill-mannered road hogs set on getting where they're going quickly—even if it kills them.

"The basic rule of thumb is just respect," says Jennifer Moses, director of operations for Funeralwise.com, a website offering free information and planning advice on all things funereal. "One should never, ever, cut into the middle of a funeral procession."

As for those in the cortege, Moses says the big rule is to follow the leader. "A (funeral home) staff member will drive the lead car and will be responsible for leading the procession through traffic lights," she says.

Here are some practical tips from Jessica A. Koth, public relations manager for the National Funeral Directors Association, on surviving a ride in a funeral procession with your dignity, your life and your automobile all intact. Koth has tips for onlookers as well.

DEGREE OF DIFFICULTY: Easy, although it can be a challenge when road hogs get in the way.

All passengers should wear seat belts.

You should follow the vehicle in front of you "as closely as is practicable and safe."

No speeding. Don't drive over 55 miles per hour on a highway with a posted speed limit of 55 or greater; drive 5 miles per hour below the posted speed on other roadways.

Turn your headlights on. The first and last vehicles in a procession should turn on their hazard lights.

When the lead car enters an intersection, the cars behind it should follow through the intersection "as long as it is safe to do so, even if the traffic light turns red." Funeral processions have the right-of-way in intersections unless an emergency vehicle approaches with lights or siren activated, or a law enforcement official directs the cortege to give up the right of way.

For drivers who encounter a funeral procession, the National Funeral Directors Association advice boils down to four simple words: Stay out of it.

Unfortunately, many motorists need to have it spelled out for them:

Do not drive between vehicles in a funeral procession unless instructed to by law enforcement personnel.

Do not join a funeral procession to secure the right of way.

Do not pass a funeral procession on the cortege's right side unless the line of vehicles is in the farthest left lane.

Do not enter an intersection, even if you have a green light, if a funeral procession is proceeding through a red light signal.

End a Relationship

There is no easy way to break up with a significant other. But you can be kind about it. Linda Young, a counseling psychologist based in Bellevue, Wash., offers advice on how to break up with someone as humanely as possible. Young is on the board of directors of the Council on Contemporary Families and runs the "Love in Limbo" blog on Psychologytoday.com.

STEP 1: WHEN TO DO IT

IDEALLY
You want to have the break-up conversation when there's plenty of time to talk in private, face-to-face, with few distractions.

THERE'S NEVER A GOOD TIME
Even if he's in a great mood, or she's had a bad day at work, don't make excuses. Decide to do it, and do it.

AN EXCEPTION
If your partner is going through something traumatic, such as a health scare or the death of a loved one, the more humane thing to do is postpone the breakup until that difficult period is over.

STEP 2: WHERE TO DO IT

IN PRIVATE
During dinner (their house may be best because then you can leave). Or have the talk while taking a walk or doing something outside in nice weather, as it's healthy to physically move when you're digesting emotional news.

IN PUBLIC
Only if you fear for your safety.

STEP 3: WHAT TO SAY

DON'T
Announce beforehand that "We need to talk."

DO
Broach the subject only when you're ready to start talking. Try: "I've been struggling with something for a while, and I'd like to come out with it..." Be honest about your reasons, but don't point fingers or declare what you don't like about your partner. Rather, say, "This is what I've discovered over time is missing." The point is that it's just a mismatch.

AVOID

Infuriating clichés, such as "It's not you, it's me" or "This is hurting me as much as it's hurting you."

STEP 4: REACTING TO THE REACTION

BE RESOLUTE

Don't backpedal and suggest you maybe can work it out, which just prolongs the inevitable.

SAY YOU'RE SORRY

Sit with your partner's tears and apologize for causing pain. If your partner gets mean and starts hurling insults, don't fight back. Just say, "I'm sorry, I know it hurts." And then listen.

STEP 5: POST-BREAKUP ETIQUETTE

Generally, it's best to cut off all contact, but you may continue to talk if your partner was shocked by the break up and needs more questions answered in order to process the situation. Follow their lead, and don't initiate contact—especially if you're second-guessing your decision—it will only cause confusion.

DEFINITELY NOT

No post-breakup sex, and don't try to be friends right away. It sends mixed signals and the dumpee may think there's a chance to get you back.

Flirting

Tell us you're not still going with "I lost my number, can I have yours?" For starters, no one loses a number in the age of smart phones. Second, seriously? You need a second reason? Time to recalibrate your approach, Mr. Cool. It'll pay off, we swear.

DEGREE OF DIFFICULTY: You must be OK with rejection as a possible outcome.

STEP 1: CHECK YOUR EGO

Understand that flirting is really not about you. "Flirting is about making the other person feel good," write Michelle Lia Lewis and Andrew Bryant in their book "Flirting 101: How to Charm Your Way to Love, Friendship and Success" (St. Martin's Griffin). "The end result is an ability to attract and hold other people's interest."

STEP 2: ADJUST YOUR ATTITUDE

"Being good-looking or clever with words is worthless if your attitude sucks," write Lewis and Bryant, who define five states of mind that ensure great flirting:

- PLAYFUL: Light-hearted, frisky, teasing
- FUN: Witty, entertaining
- AWARE: Takes notice of the other person, shows interest
- CURIOUS: Loves people, gregarious, social
- BRAVE: Goes for it, takes risks, optimistic, opportunistic

STEP 3: START TALKING

Check your posture—shoulders back, chin up. Make eye contact. Talk. Start with open-ended questions: "What do you think about..." Move into bolder territory: "If you could get on a plane right now, where would you go?" "Ever lied to pick up someone?" "Any tattoos or secret piercings?" Say nothing while the person is talking, and pause before responding, so the person knows he or she is being heard. "Once you are deep in conversation," say the "Flirting 101" folks, "make eye contact regularly and hold their gaze for just a few seconds longer than usual. This has a real impact." But beware: "Any longer than a few extra seconds and you'll risk weirding them out."

STEP 4: FLATTER

Your flirting partner will probably lob a question or two your way. Before you dive in with an answer, lay on some charm. "Wow, great question. What made you ask me that?" Then pay a genuine compliment. But be specific—none of that "You're really sweet" or "You're the best" nonsense. Think clothes ("That top is great on you"); gestures ("It's so cute the way you play with your hair"); qualities ("You're a great conversationalist").

STEP 5: SEAL THE DEAL

If you're being well received so far, get a little physical: Lightly touch an arm. Take a step closer. Lean. At this rate, you may just get that number after all.

DO NOT

- Flirt in front of people you or they know
- Stay close by if they're not interested
- Drink a lot before flirting

Get Your Foot in the Door

Desperate to get your kid educated, your appeal granted, your screenplay read? There are so many gatekeepers in life, so few open gates.

Among the barriers to entry is the receptionist. Despite that title, when you ask, you rarely receive, at least not what you want to hear. The question is: How do you get past the rejectionist, and get an answer, good or bad, from the boss?

"Say: 'Look over there!' And then when the receptionist is distracted, bolt through the door," jokes Kerry Patterson, co-author of "Change Anything" (Business Plus) and other leadership books.

Still, getting over the stone wall requires some bravado. "You have to be a little aggressive," said Ellen Lubin-Sherman, author of "The Essentials of Fabulous" (Launch). "It's a game. You have to play to win."

DEGREE OF DIFFICULTY: Hard

WHAT YOU NEED: Chutzpah, resilience, organization

STEP 1

Call and ask politely to schedule a meeting with the principal/employer/supervisor. Briefly state your agenda, framed in a way that repels an easy rejection or referral to a website.

So, instead of "I'd like to schedule a meeting with Ms. Ross about job opportunities"—to which the receptionist may reply, "There are no openings at this time"—try something like, "I'd like to schedule a meeting with Ms. Ross to discuss ideas I have for enhancing your website and increasing your revenue."

IF THE REQUEST IS REBUFFED:

STEP 2

Plot a schedule of follow-up calls, and keep a record.

"Put on the calendar when you called the person and call back six days later or leave a short voice mail," Lubin-Sherman said. "Never ask the person to call you back. It's not going to happen. Say, 'Sorry I missed you; I am going to call you back next Wednesday at 2. I hope that's convenient.' When the clock strikes 2 on Wednesday, you'd better be on the phone calling."

Even if they screen the call, "these are meta-messages that communicate you are really serious about this," Lubin-Sherman said. "Pace yourself, and never let it get to the point where you're a nuisance."

STEP 3

Some may find this objectionable, but Lubin-Sherman suggests that if you haven't gotten through yet, "pick up the phone and tell the receptionist you are returning the (boss's) phone call." She doesn't view this as a lie, but as part of the game. "Receptionists are trained to screen out all calls," she said. The boss might just be impressed if you penetrate the force field.

STEP 4

Find a way to "run into" the decision-maker. A business trick is to find out where the target has lunch or an association she belongs to and go there. Or—"this is really sort of out there, but I know people who have done it," Patterson said—park near the target's parking lot.

As he arrives, cordially and quickly make your case. It may smack of stalking, "but your intentions are good," Patterson said. "You're trying to work it into their free time."

PARTING ADVICE

Remember, it pays to be proactive, Patterson said. On the recent first day of a business class that he teaches at Brigham Young University, he said one unregistered student approached him at the start, despite the fact the class was officially full, and pointed to an empty seat. So Patterson told the student to tell the department receptionist he had given permission for the student to join if no one was sick.

"I always admire chutzpah, rather than someone who mails in a resume and accepts an easy rejection," Patterson said. "It might be more annoying when it happens, but I have a bias for action."

Give a Wedding Toast

For the legions of best men and maids of honor stumped about what to say, Tom Haibeck—author of "Wedding Toasts Made Easy"—offers some tips for preparing and delivering a gorgeous toast.

DO

- Make it personal. Identify three anecdotes that are humorous or illustrate something the audience might not know about the bride or groom.
- Use gentle humor, but be mindful of your audience (don't offend grandma).
- Rehearse, ideally in the venue.
- Exercise the day of the wedding to work off any nervous energy.
- End your toast with a positive comment about the couple, and raise your glass.

DO NOT

- Exceed five minutes. Ideally, a toast should be two to three minutes.
- Try to be funny if you're not.
- Have a drink to calm your nerves. One drink often leads to another and before you know it you're sloshed.
- Write out your speech and read it word for word. Instead, jot down some key points on index cards.
- Rely on canned wedding toasts you buy off the Internet.

Have a Tough Conversation

When the stakes of a conversation are high, many of us clam up or blow up. A recent survey by Al Switzler, Kerry Patterson, Joseph Grenny and Ron McMillan, co-authors of "Crucial Conversations: Tools for Talking When Stakes Are High" (McGraw-Hill), found that the person most people struggle to hold difficult, life-changing conversations with is their boss. Spouses are second. In the survey, 525 respondents identified a single conversation that had life-altering consequences. More than half said the effects of this one conversation lasted forever. Nearly two-thirds permanently damaged a relationship. One in seven harmed a career.

The authors arrived at the main reasons for failure in a crucial conversation: inability to control emotions, not gaining the other person's trust, and getting defensive, vengeful or fearful.

Fearing those foibles, many stay mum. People think that hunkering down in silence will save their job or marriage or family harmony. But co-author Switzler said, "When problems linger, you get rigidity and reduced respect. Those are big costs. If you can catch problems and do it in a way that's civil and courteous, you outperform the competition.

"This is not about holding hands and singing campfire songs, or having a good talk. This is all about putting the toughest issues on the table so you can rapidly and respectfully resolve them." Here's how:

STEP 1: REVERSE YOUR THINKING.

Consider the risk of not speaking up. One survey by the authors, involving managers and employees at various companies, found that the cost of not holding a crucial conversation, on average, is about $1,500 and eight hours of an employee's time, spent on avoidance tactics and gossip. Another survey found that, in families that haven't addressed a high-stakes issue, they can be together for just an hour and a half before there's an outburst.

Rather than broaching the conversation as a confrontation in which one person wins, ask yourself, "What can I do to resolve the issue AND strengthen the relationship?" Switzler said.

STEP 2: HELP OTHERS FEEL SAFE.

Assure the other party of your positive intentions and respect. Family members, in particular, know where the hot buttons are. "And when the adrenaline fires, with the moral certainty that 'it's my time to win!' they can argue in bad ways," Switzler said.

"If you have your intentions right before you open your mouth, and you get a response that's not helpful, you can call timeout. Say 'Whoa, I wasn't trying to do that, I was trying to do this.' There are timeout and retreat tactics that help give people the confidence to put issues on the table. It's not like you only get one roll of the dice."

STEP 3: OFFER OBSERVATIONS AND QUESTIONS, NOT EMOTIONS AND CONCLUSIONS.

Stick to the heart of the issue and focus on long-term goals for the conversation and relationship, e.g., "We agreed before we changed a deadline we would give our team two days' notice. On the last two occasions we've only had about six hours. Can we talk about it so that we can keep up performance and morale?" Even if the person holds views you oppose, separate the problem from the person.

EMOTIONS CAN TRIGGER ADRENALINE.

"That puts blood into fight-or-flight muscles so that, when it matters the most, our brain gets blood-starved and dumbed down," Switzler said. If you feel that happening, redirect blood to your brain with this thought: "Why would a reasonable, rational, decent person do this?" he suggests. It gives the person the benefit of the doubt. "Whether a boss or a child or a stranger, if you could learn to lead with observations and questions, you can talk to anybody about anything."

Picking Up the Check

Who pays for dinner on the first date? On the third? What if the event is an evening out with relatives, a birthday celebration or an impromptu office outing? Deborah King, president of Final Touch Finishing School in Seattle, clears up the confusion.

DATING

FIRST DATE
Whoever issues the invitation picks up the tab. It doesn't matter if you're male or female, going out for lunch or dinner. If you asked, you pay.

SECOND DATE
The second date goes by the same principle as the first.

THIRD DATE
Sometime around the third date, the person who is not paying may want to start chipping in. A gracious way to indicate this might be to say, "I'll buy the tickets for the show, why don't you pick up the tab for dinner?" Or go ahead and purchase tickets ahead of time for a sporting event you know your date will enjoy.

Similarly, there may come a point where the person who has been paying wants to split expenses more evenly. A polite way to broach this topic is to pick a time when you're both comfortable and ask a gentle, hypothetical question, maybe, "What do you think about the woman sometimes picking up the tab?" If the answer is along the lines of, "I'd never stand for that," you may not want to pursue the topic. If the answer is more favorable, press on.

32ND DATE

Some women never, ever feel comfortable paying, and King says that's perfectly fine—if communication is good and both love-birds are on the same page.

DOUBLE DATE

The couple that does the inviting pays. If you're not paying, it's a nice gesture to cover the tip.

PARTIES

BIRTHDAY PARTY

The restaurant birthday party can be a socially ambiguous affair. Who's hosting: the birthday girl or the best friend who made the reservation? Still, King points out, "somebody had to put the word out" that the event was taking place. This person may not be the host in the classic sense, but he or she is the person to whom you can address the relevant question, "Are we all chipping in?"

GROUP OF CO-WORKERS

Again, it's a good idea to ask upfront and be clear about who is paying. Faced with the dreaded splitting of the bill, King likes to estimate her share, rather than doing elaborate calculations, and to err on the side of generosity. The worst thing that can happen when you take that approach, she says, is that the server gets a bonus.

FAMILY AFFAIR

Just because you're the one organizing the periodic night out, complete with in-laws and uncles, doesn't mean that you have to foot the bill. Everyone does their part financially, just as everyone would help out (bringing dessert, clearing the table) if they were eating at your home.

OUT-OF-TOWN GUEST

It's a nice thank-you gesture for the guest to pay for a restaurant meal.

ONE MORE THING

Congratulations! Now you know the rules. Unfortunately, your dining companions may not. Always prepare for this possibility, King says. For instance, bring enough money (or the appropriate credit card) on a first date, even if you were not the one who issued the invitation.

Someone's Fly is Down

You encounter a poor, zipper-challenged person in a public place. Should you say something? And if so, how? Here's a guide to the delicate art of the open-fly alert, compiled with the help of John Bridges, author of "How to be a Gentleman," and Curtrise Garner, author of "The New Rules of Etiquette: A Young Woman's Guide to Style and Poise at Work, at Home, and on the Town."

STEP 1: SURVEY THE SCENE

TELL
If you're on a crowded bus, at work, at a party or other social gathering, then, prepare to deliver the bad news.

DON'T TELL
If there are a lot of people within earshot, see Step #3. If you're just passing someone on the street or at the grocery store, don't bother.

STEP 2: DO YOU DO THE TELLING?

Generally, most people would rather be slightly mortified now than more mortified later, so assume they want to know. So go for it, but beware of these caveats:

OPPOSITE GENDER

If the unzipped is a person of the opposite gender and he/she could be embarrassed by that, ask someone of the victim's same gender to deliver the news.

BOSS

If it's the CEO of your company or a potential employer, it's probably best to feign ignorance and wait for someone else to tell.

NEWLY ACQUAINTED

Better to ask the person who introduced you to tell your target about his/her open fly.

STEP 3: BREAKING THE NEWS

PULL THEM ASIDE

Ideally, pull the person to the side or to a corner where he/she can make the fix, and tell them in a low whisper, "Your fly is unzipped" or, "I think you might want to check your fly."

PASS BY

If you can't pull them to the side, pass by them and whisper in their ear that their fly is open. Do it quickly and don't make a big deal about it. Walk away.

IF THEY LAUGH

Only then may you laugh at the situation.

IF THEY'RE ANGRY

Say, "Hey, I'm sorry, I was just trying to be helpful."

The Social Kiss

Right cheek or left? Actual or simulated contact? Single or double? In all its iterations, the social kiss is spreading across the U.S. like pollen in spring—warmly welcomed by some; dodged like an allergen by others.

"It's become such an affectation, with the proliferation of all these reality shows," says socialprimer.com blogger K. Cooper Ray, who has lived in New York, Milan, Los Angeles and now Charleston, S.C., where social kissing is not customary.

"It is cultural," said etiquette heiress Anna Post, and not just a matter of France to New York, but rather "family to family and block to block and social group to social group."

Michael Callahan has seen his share of social smooching as deputy editor at Town & Country magazine. He comes out in favor of it despite the often-clumsy execution. "I would argue in the scheme of things that it is better to vote for more warmth and conviviality than less," he said.

Our experts offer novices some best practices to avoid the worst-case scenario: meeting in the middle of a social kiss. "Lip to lip, a lot of people would sooner fall through the floor," Post said.

DEGREE OF DIFFICULTY: High and mighty! (The cost if flubbed: social ruin!)

KNOW WHERE YOU ARE

In most American cities, if administered at all, a social kiss typically consists of a single, right cheek to right cheek. Europeans and New Yorkers often double kiss, first right cheek, then left. The double is Ray's preference, but he reserves it for actual friends, male and female, except in the South. "Social kissing a Southern man? It just would not happen ever, ever, ever, ever," he said. In Los Angeles, the social kiss is employed even in business, man to man—"the Hollywood executive kind of thing," Ray observes. It's also a tool for social climbers there, where "proximity to power equals power, and a social kiss is an easy tool of ingratiation."

AVOID UNDUE FORCE.

Ray suggests that "both hands lightly grasp the target's elbows for balance and then each turns to present right cheeks first, then left, where dry, glancing contact is made"—via a quick twist of the mouth. (A London paper teased Naomi Campbell for an ungainly approach in an air kiss, with the caption, "Come here, you!") Post finds no fault in pressing just cheeks, without lip-to-cheek contact. All three experts view a lean-in with zero contact as pretentious, and agree that a sloppy, wet kiss is equally offensive.

SOUND OR SILENCE?

Post says her godmother often sends a "mwah" air kiss from across the kitchen if she's elbow deep in food prep when Post arrives. Post likes that just fine. Ray dislikes the stereotypical nose-in-the-air "mwah-mwah." Callahan also prefers no sound effects.

SECONDS.

When dealing with a European, turn the other cheek for a second kiss. In America, if you're brazen enough to initiate a double, Ray suggests whispering "so good to see you" or "how are you" to dissipate any awkwardness. Some skip a second kiss and hug it out instead, which Ray often finds falsely intimate, reminiscent of Ari on the HBO show "Entourage." Post likes a single kiss followed by an upper-body hug. Follow your partner's cues.

ALTERNATIVES

The nod. A smile and nod in greeting is always correct, K. Cooper Ray said.

A handshake is almost always appropriate, Anna Post said.

The hug. In U.S. cities, the new norm seems to be a handshake or nod upon introduction, then, at the end of the social encounter, an upper-body hug or single social kiss if you have conversed at some length, Michael Callahan said.

Tip for Services

Tipping is a favorite pastime in America, where nothing says "thank you" like a few dollar bills. But there is often a moment, after you get your car washed, or your furniture delivered, or your flat tire changed, when suddenly a wave of anxiety strikes. Are you supposed to tip? And if so, how much?

Here's a guide to what's customary for tipping in the U.S., compiled using information from the Emily Post Institute (emilypost.com), The Original Tipping Page (tipping.org) and "The New Rules of Etiquette," by Curtrise Garner.

And remember: "The whole point is to thank the person," said Peggy Post, great-granddaughter-in-law of etiquette maven Emily Post and director of the Emily Post Institute. "Instead of just throwing a dollar bill at someone, the key thing is to say 'thank you.'"

RESTAURANTS

- Waiter: 15 percent to 20 percent (pre-tax)
- Buffet: 10 percent
- Bartender: $1 per drink or 15 percent to 20 percent of the bar tab
- Takeout: No need, but 10 percent for special favors
- Host or maitre d': No need, but $10-$20 on occasion if you're a regular patron
- Sommelier: 15 percent of the cost of the wine

- Restroom attendant: 50 cents-$3, depending on the service
- Cloakroom attendant: $1 per coat
- Food delivery person: 10 percent of bill (pre-tax); $2 minimum
- Valet: $2-$5

HOTELS

- Doorman: $1-$2 for carrying luggage; $1-$2 for hailing a cab; $1-$4 for going beyond the call of duty
- Bellhop: $2 first bag, $1 per additional bag
- Housekeeper: $2-$5 per day, left daily in an envelope or with a note clearly marked for the maid
- Concierge: $5 for tickets or reservations, $10 if they're hard to get

Turn Down a Request

Rejecting a request generally isn't fun, whether the advance is romantic ("Want to go out Saturday?"), professional ("Can you have the report done by 1 p.m.?") or social ("Come on, just one more drink!").

"A lot of times people say yes when they don't want to, because they're afraid of hurting or disappointing somebody," said Ben Benjamin, co-author with Amy Yeager and Anita Simon of the forthcoming book, "Conversation Transformation: Recognize and Overcome the 6 Most Destructive Communication Patterns" (McGraw-Hill).

"People worry, 'What will happen if I say no?'" added Yeager. "They have a worst-case scenario in their head."

Here's how to avoid regretting your response.

DEGREE OF DIFFICULTY: Hard—if you have trouble saying no. But, like most things, it gets easier with practice.

BUY TIME.

"There is a whole group of people who immediately say no without thinking and another who say yes without thinking," Benjamin said. "I give the same advice to both groups: 'Thanks for asking. Let me think about it.' Then think about, 'What do I want from this situation?'"

You need to know your tendencies. That self-awareness can help you avoid a knee-jerk response in either direction.

Out of courtesy, give them a time frame, Yeager said. "'Let me look at my schedule and I'll get back to you in an hour, or tomorrow.' They're not left hanging."

BEWARE OF OFFERS YOU CAN'T REFUSE.

Sometimes, a request isn't a direct, open question. Your acceptance is assumed. "I want to watch the games today (so you will be in charge of the kids for the next 10 hours)." Or, "You did such a great job with x, we've given you the honor of y!" That can create feelings of manipulation, which leads to arguing or resentment.

"Understand what the leading question is—it's a question AND it's an opinion telling you what the right answer is," Benjamin said. A strategy for dealing with it is to paraphrase what you heard. "I hear you saying you want to watch the games; are you asking if I will keep the kids busy till bedtime?" That gives you time to think, "Am I all right with this?" If not, say, "I had a different idea; let's talk about it."

AVOID AMBIGUITY.

If someone asks if you'd like to go out, and you aren't interested, skip the procrastination and mixed messages. "It's often easier in the long run to be direct. Not cruel, but direct," Yeager said. If there's a real reason you feel comfortable sharing, you can add one briefly.

"No matter what you're saying, keep your voice tone neutral and clear," Yeager said. "Be clear with yourself in what you're saying and not have guilt or worry come through." Added Benjamin: "If you do a 'yes, but,' the person is going to come back again and again, and it's even more disappointing and upsetting, and you get caught in a lie."

Intending to demonstrate goodwill, people often respond with a sort of yes-no-yes, as in, "Oh, bowling sounds like such fun. But I told my mom I would take her shopping and then I have to do carpool and then Allie hasn't been feeling well. I wish I could join you." If you have no intention of ever heaving a bowling ball, you've just delayed the inevitable letdown. If the person sees through your veil of regret, you've called your sincerity into question for future interactions.

Living in reality is ultimately easier, Benjamin said, even if occasionally uncomfortable: "People often think they have to lie, otherwise the person is going to be mad." And sometimes they will.

But, he said, "Both business and interpersonal relationships fail when people are behaving in ways that are not resonant with what they want."

CREDITS

Illustrations by Rick Tuma except on pages 49, 95, and 159 (illustrations on those pages by Casey Millard).

CHICAGO TRIBUNE ARTICLES

The following articles are listed by the order in which they appear.

Hageman, William. "Arrange Flowers." September 26, 2010.

Hevrdejs, Judy. "Clean a Bathroom." July 1, 2011.

Hevrdejs, Judy. "Clean the Refrigerator." Sunday, November 21, 2010.

Elejalde-Ruiz, Alexia. "Cut Your Own Hair." February 8, 2012.

Schoenberg, Nara. "Decode Nutritional Labels." August 25, 2010.

Elejalde-Ruiz, Alexia. "Hang a Painting." February 8, 2011.

Mahany, Barbara. "Iron a Shirt." June 12, 2010.

Hageman, William. "Make a Good Sign." February 23, 2011.

Schoenberg, Nara. "Pick Fruit." November 14, 2010.

Daley, Bill. "Plant a Tree." April 4, 2012.

Mahany, Barbara. "Polish Your Nails." May 28, 2010.

Mahany, Barbara. "Repot a Houseplant." March 21, 2012.

Hevrdejs, Judy. "Sew a Button." December 26, 2010.

Hageman, William. "Shine Leather Shoes." August 22, 2010.

Hageman, William. "Snuff a Kitchen Fire." January 25, 2011.

Donahue, Wendy. "Tie a Bow Tie." March 28, 2010.

Hageman, William "Wash a Dog." May 2, 2010.

Hageman, William. "Wash a Window." April 6, 2011.

Hevrdejs, Judy. "Wash a Wine Glass." January 11, 2012.

Schoenberg, Nara. "Wrap a Gift." November 16, 2011.

Elejalde-Ruiz, Alexia. "Ask for a Raise." September 12, 2010.

Wendy Donahue. "Clean a Computer Keyboard." August 14, 2011.

Williams, Kevin. "Clean Your Desk." December 28, 2010.

Elejalde-Ruiz, Alexia. "DIY Facial Massage." October 5, 2011.

Hageman, William. "Avoid Dog Bites." May 31, 2011.

Stevens, Heidi, "Babysit a 1-Year-Old." March 21, 2010.

Elejalde-Ruiz, Alexia. "Bowl Without Hurting Anyone." March 7, 2012.

Cavendish, Steve. "Grab a Cab." January 12, 2011.

Hageman, William. "Keep Score at the Ballpark." March 23, 2011.

Noel, Josh. "Make Outfield Grass Patterns at Home." June 20, 2010.

Hageman, William. "Pack for Road Trips." May 1, 2011.

Hageman, William. "Photograph a Dog." May 1, 2012.

Hevrdejs, Judy. "Prepare an Evacuation Kit." November 1, 2011.

Mahany, Barbara. "Summer First Aid for Kids." June 5, 2010.

Stevens, Heidi. "Teach Bike Riding." August 1, 2010.

Elejalde-Ruiz, Alexia. "Change a Tire." October 21, 2011.

Hageman, William. "Critical Car Checks." April 11, 2010.

Elejalde-Ruiz, Alexia. "Display the American Flag." May 16, 2012.

Mahany, Barbara. "Fix a Leaky Faucet." December 13, 2011.

Elejalde-Ruiz, Alexia. "Jump Start a Car Battery." August 24, 2011.

Hageman, William. "Load a Truck on Moving Day." September 7, 2011.

Elejalde-Ruiz, Alexia. "Make Campfire Without Matches." June 19, 2011.

Daley, Bill. "Smarter Lawn Mowing." May 22, 2011.

Hageman, William. "Take/Throw a Punch." October 10, 2010.

Mahany, Barbara. "Unclog a Bathroom Drain." July 13, 2011.

Donahue, Wendy. "Apologize." January 24, 2012.

Schoenberg, Nara. "Ask for a Favor." April 18, 2012.

Daley, Bill. "Be a Good Witness to a Crime." March 8, 2011.

Elejalde-Ruiz, Alexia. "Break the Ice." November 29, 2011.

Stevens, Heidi. "Choose an Engagement Ring." June 30, 2010.

Schoenberg, Nara. "Door Etiquette." April 3, 2010.

Daley, Bill. "Drive in a Funeral." July 27, 2011.

Elejalde-Ruiz, Alexia. "End a Relationship." May 22, 2010.

Stevens, Heidi. "Flirting." April 18, 2010.

Donahue, Wendy. "Get Your Foot in the Door." September 20, 2011.

Elejalde-Ruiz, Alexia. "Give a Wedding Toast." April 24, 2012.

Donahue, Wendy. "Have a Tough Conversation." December 27, 2011.

Schoenberg, Nara. 'Picking Up the Check." October 24, 2010.

Elejalde-Ruiz, Alexia. "Someone's Fly is Down." May 6, 2010.

Donahue, Wendy. "The Social Kiss." May 4, 2011.

Elejalde-Ruiz, Alexia. "Tip for Services." May 13, 2010.

Donahue, Wendy. "Turn Down a Request." February 21, 2012.